Price Guide

African and Asian Costumed Dolls

Second in Series

by Polly and Pam Judd

Published by Hobby House Press, Inc.
Grantsville, Maryland 21536

DEDICATION

The authors dedicate this book to the companies and individual people who through the years have helped the indigenous people of the world help themselves by making dolls of their cultures for commercial sale. Companies such as Kimport, Elsie Krug, and World-Wide Doll Club have introduced both children and doll collectors to the cultures of the world. For 40 years the Brimful House of Boynton Beach, Florida has been supplying work to families in Africa and India. They are still selling these handcrafted products today. The Readshaw/MacMillan Trading, Ltd. of Thailand has been helping the Hilltribes of Thailand help themselves and yet preserve their cultural heritage. Recently, among their engineering projects for the Hilltribes, they are supporting a project to teach the tribes to make their colorful dolls commercially viable. There are many others such as Serrv that also help people help themselves. The authors salute you all.

ACKNOWLEDGEMENTS

As usual this book contains the pictures and dolls from many people who helped and believed in our global philosophy: Shirley Karaba and Sandy Strater not only supplied dolls, but they also shared long hours of animated talk about how best to present the unusual dolls in this book. Sherry Morgan from Florida, a world traveler, sent pictures and research from many parts of the world. Bill Zito from Wisconsin sent pictures of dolls and spent hours on the phone discussing their costumes and the research he had done on each one. Susan Hendrick and the Rosalie Whyel Museum from Washington State provided pictures of museum dolls. Gigi Williams of Illinois, long time friend, went out of her way to send us rare dolls. Yoshiko Baker, a Japanese doll artist from Ohio, supplied first hand knowledge of Japanese dolls both old and new, and photographs of her dolls, some of which are a century or more old. Harriet Beerbas of California sent her remarkable African photography.

Others that shared their dolls are: Carlton Brown, Barbara and Jim Comieniski, Jackie Dukes, Beverly Findlay, Jean Horton, Marge Hunter, Shirley Lindner, Mary Jane's Dolls, Amy Miller, Eleanor Niles, Louise Schnell, Tanya Secrest, Mary Tanner and Pat Morsuk.

Ninety year old Thema Purvis provided pictures for this book, but we also want to salute her for establishing a small museum in the Cleveland Heights library containing hundreds of dolls from around the world. There are always smiling children sitting in front of the cases asking their teachers or parents wonderful questions about the people of the world.

Finally we would like to thank our editor Mary Beth Ruddell for unfailing patience, kindness and her ability to make "things work"!

Front Cover: See pages 22 and 114 for more information on these dolls.
Title Page: See page 132 for more information about this doll.
Back Cover: See pages 20 and 77 for more information on these dolls.

African & Asian Costumed Dolls is an independent study by the authors Polly & Pam Judd and published by Hobby House Press, Inc. The research and publication of this book were not sponsored in any way by the manufacturers of the dolls, the doll costumes and the doll accessories featured in this study. Photographs of the collectibles were from dollls, costumes or accessories belonging to Polly or Pam Judd at the time the picture was taken unless otherwise credited with the caption.

The information as to the ownership pertains to documentary materials contemporary with the doll or doll's accessories. Ownership of the registered trademark, the trademark or the copyright may have expired or been transferred to another owner.

The values given within this book are intended as value guides rather than arbitrarily set prices. The values quoted are as accurate as possible but in the case of errors, typographical, clerical or otherwise, the authors and publisher assume no liability nor responsibility for any loss incurred by users of this book.

Additional copies of this book may be purchased at $14.95 (plus postage and handling) from

Hobby House Press, Inc.
1 Corporate Drive
Grantsville, Maryland 21536
1-800-554-1447
or from your favorite bookstore or dealer.

©1995 Pam & Polly Judd

All rights reserved. No part of this book may be reproduced or utilized in any form or by any means, electronic or mechanical, including photocopying, recording, or by any information storage and retrieval system, without permission in writing from the publisher. Inquiries should be addressed to Hobby House Press, Inc., 1 Corporate Drive, Grantsville, Maryland 21536.

Printed in the United States of America.

ISBN: 0-87588-445-8

Table Of Contents

Foreword 4
System Used for Pricing Dolls 4
Price Guide 164
When referencing a country they are alphabetically arranged under specific continent.
When referencing a price they are alphabetically arranged by country.
Index 174
Costumed Dolls From:

AFRICA

Algeria 6
Benin 7
Botswana 8
Burkina Faso (formerly Upper Volta) 9
Egypt 10
Ethiopia 13
Ghana 15
Ivory Coast 22
Kenya 17
Lesotho 21
Libya 23
Madagascar 23
Malawi 24
Morocco 25
Natal 29
Namibia 30
Nigeria 31
South Africa 33
Tanzania 37
Tunisia 39
West Africa 41
Zaire 42
Zambia 44
Zanzibar 45
Zimbabwe (Old Rhodesia) 46

ASIA

Afghanistan 49
Banglasdesh 51
Burma (Mynamar) 52
China 53
Hong Kong 71
India 74
Indonesia (Java, Bali) 85
Iran 89
Iraq 90
Israel 91
Japan 95
Jordan 121
Korea and Viet Nam 124
Kuwait 128
Laos 129
Lebanon 130
Malaysia 131
Mongolia 132
Nepal 133
Pakistan 135
Saudi Arabia 137
Singapore 138
Sri Lanka (formerly Ceylon) 140
Syria 141
Taiwan 143
Thailand 147
Tibet 156
Turkey 157
Yemen 162

FORWARD

This is the second in the trilogy of books about the costumes and cultures of people around the world. Although the standard worldwide clothes may be "tops and pants," we have researched and presented the traditional costumes and customs of the African and Asian countries. We have discovered that people around the world are becoming more educated, more mobile, more automated, with televisions and computers escalating, and interest building for the "Information Highway."

Doll collectors are suddenly interested in international costume dolls, and people like Loretta Nardone, a doll author and teacher, are winning awards for creating school study guides using dolls as a way to understand other people and hopefully make a better world.

Many people the world over are concerned with the knowledge of their genealogy, their heritage, and their old ways of life. They strive to leave the legacy of past generations for future generations. What better way to preserve history than by collecting and treasuring the international dolls of the past and present!

Our objectives in this book are daunting. Africa and Asia present two entirely different ways of life. Japan, for instance, has been making and preserving dolls since about 500 A.D. while an African doll 100 years old is a national treasure.

In all our books we have tried to show both expensive and inexpensive dolls from various time periods. Again we say, "This type of collecting is for everyone who loves the people around the world."

SYSTEM USED FOR PRICING DOLLS

There has been a fluctuating rise in the price of International dolls in the doll market recently because of the interest by many doll collectors in their own heritage as well as preserving the legacies of different cultures around the world. There is a strong market for International dolls in their original condition, clothes, and if possible, in their original boxes.

An example brought to the authors' attention was an Indonesian puppet doll (see page 86 top left). Just six months ago the owner purchased the doll for $60 which she thought was quite high. In the last month the same type of doll, in the same condition was auctioned for $400. Our experience is that this is not an isolated event.

Just before World War II, mail order houses such as Kimport were doing thriving business with both inexpensive and expensive dolls. An example from this era is the doll on page 26, bottom left, which was sold for $5. It was recently purchased for $300. The reader should remember that these extreme price increases are still not the norm.

For this reason, the pricing of the dolls pictured in this book will reflect a wider range of prices than is usual.

Two areas in particular have widely accelerating prices: the art dolls from Japan and Africa.

There are cycles in collecting, and at this time there seems to be a rising appreciation of International dolls. Again, like dolls from other eras and materials, prices rise and fall. However, in talking to dealers, monitoring auction prices, etc., it is getting very hard to predict prices of the "souvenirs" of the past as accurately as could be done even a year ago.

In this book the price variation also includes "good to tissue-mint-in box" dolls. Dolls in poor condition will be about one third to one half of the lowest price.

The dolls in this book are different from other books. While most of them cannot be called rare dolls, they have a way of increasing in their value as they are identified and people understand their place in history.

AFRICA

See page 37 for more information about this doll.

ALGERIA

Algeria is the second largest nation in Africa. Bordering the Mediterranean Sea, it has a fertile coastal area called the Tell (hill) – a high plateau region where cattle, sheep, and goats graze, and a desolate area where it abuts the Sahara. This type of geography as well as a history of invasions over the centuries, promotes a diverse population.

Along the coast, many of the people wear Western clothes although the Muslim influence is still important, as the men can be seen wearing the fez with a business suit, or a long hooded gown called a Burnouse of linen in the summer and wool in the winter. The women may wear Western clothes with a small white or black veil over their lower face only. A long Muslim overgarment, called a heik, may also be worn to cover the woman's body and most of the face.

In the Tuareg villages men wrap five yards of indigo blue material around the head into a turban that also goes over their robes and hides all but their eyes. The Tuareg women cover their heads but not their faces in the turn-about fashion. The women dominate rather than the men, controlling the economy and property.

The great majority of the land is desert, with caravans of camels transporting nomadic people and their goods for sale.

Almost every Algerian is a Muslim of Arab, Berber, or mixed descent. However, everyone does not follow Islamic rules, especially in the larger cities.

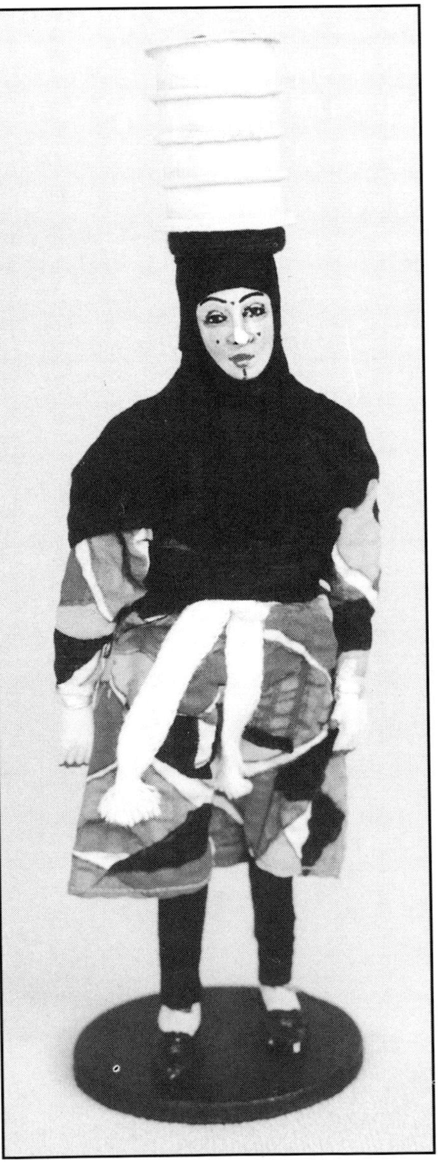

#1. Algerian Woman Carrying Round Boxes: 9.5in (24cm); painted plaster face, hands, feet; cloth body; varied-colored triangular print dress; black scarf over dress and head; white belt; narrow black leggings; black Kohl dots tattooed on cheeks and forehead as the dolls on page 40; black eyebrows. Purchased at the United Nations in 1966.
MARKS: None on Doll.

1

BENIN

The original inhabitants of this kingdom called themselves, their capital, and language "Edo." Most of today's people still do. Benin is a very small country between Nigeria and Bukina Faso. An important art country, Benin has various metal resources. From the beginning of their civilization, natives made their art figures in both bronze and brass. They became very skilled artisans, and their art, unlike the wooden art of other African countries, survived to tell much of their history. They have passed their metal technology from generation to generation, and today still have skilled artisans making similar art pieces.

#2. Dignitary Holding Ceremonial Sword: 11in (28cm); brass; excellent detail; fashioned after the original brasses from the 17th century. Figure was created after World War II by the old lost wax method of brass casting which requires a metal alloy (brass alloys are copper and zinc), pure beeswax, and clay mixed with different organic substances, such as goat's hair or chaff for the mold. The actual technique is time consuming, and there are several methods that are used for the desired result.
MARKS: None.

2

BOTSWANA

Two-thirds of Botswana is the vast Kalahari desert, one of the driest deserts in the world. In spite of precipitation problems, Botswana has managed to maintain high economic growth due to land adaptation and the discovery of diamond mines. Diverse tribes and differing life styles, has left Botswana with a history of racial inequality. Today, Botswana is an independent nation well on its way to becoming one of the most modern nations in Africa.

Most inhabitants wear the type of modern clothes required for hot weather conditions. The Herero women continue to wear long, brightly colored dresses with many petticoats and matching turbans as seen on left. This fashion began with the missionaries.

Their handicrafts are among the world's finest. Colorful dolls preserve their culture and build income.

3

#3. Herero Doll: 10in (25cm); all cloth; quilt-type dress of Botswana fabrics; black shawl; white inverted canoe-shaped hat. *Jackie Dukes Collection.*
MARKS: "Herero Doll//Botswana."

#4. Botswana Lady: 14.5in (37cm); stuffed cloth head and body; wood buttocks and legs; blue cloth wrappings; cloth arms hidden under ochre colored leather cape with blue and yellow beading; matching hat with three beaded panels and three upright strips; blue beaded necklace; old zipper pieces wrapped around each ankle for decoration; 1994. Purchased at U.N.I.C.E.F. store in Albuquerque, New Mexico; 1990. *Sherry Morgan Collection.*
MARKS: None.

4

BURKINA FASO *(formerly Upper Volta)*

Burkina Faso, one of the newly named countries of Western Africa, is north of Ghana, and the Ivory Coast; south and east of Mali; west of Niger, Benin, and Togo.

First settled by African farmers living along the southern trade routes, the war-like Mossi people tried to conquer Mali, but failed and blended with the farmers. In 1919 the French united several states into their colony of Upper Volta. In 1984 it became an independent country and changed its name to Burkina Faso. They are a poor country struggling to educate their people and move into the 21st century. Their language is French.

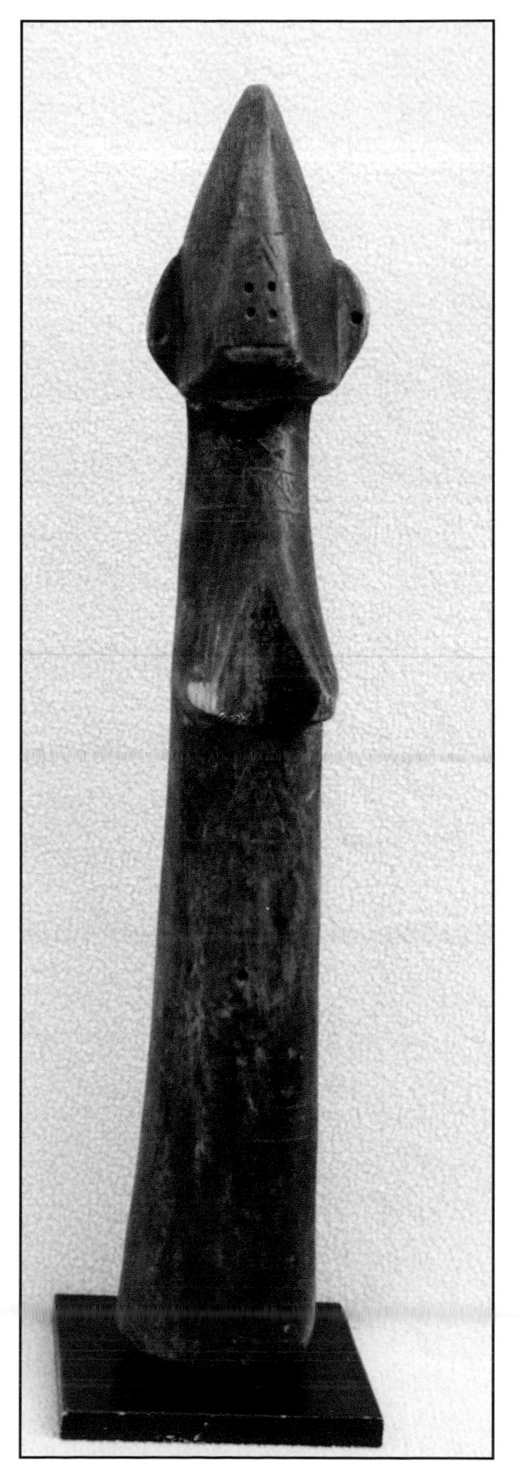

#5. Upper Volta Mossi Doll: 10in (25cm); all wood figure; very primitive design; carvings on neck and triangular head; 1950s–1960s.
MARKS: None.

5

EGYPT

The Nile River flows eternally through the sands of Egypt as dolls reflect the unique blend of Egypt's ancient civilizations and the more recent culture of the Arabs. Dolls are not as common in Egypt as in Europe or the United States. Interesting, inexpensive and different dolls from historical Egypt are difficult to find. Most of the available dolls for tourists to bring home are men and women dressed in caftans that are worn in the desert countries of the Near East. However, once in a while an unknown doll maker can be found on the side of a road where the buses pass. Most of the dolls are very primitive, but a few are pieces of art. Beautiful dolls can also be found in fashionable boutiques, museum shops and bazaar stalls.

6

#6. Egyptian Couple: 10in (25cm) woman; 11in (28cm) man; heavy cloth with expressive features; common dress. The woman wears a translucent veil and a large gold necklace, typical of Egyptian jewelry. The man wears a shawl and carries touch beads in his hand. Purchased in the gift shop of the Egyptian Museum in Cairo.
MARKS: Egyptian Doll//Onnig Alixanian//Egyptian Museum//Cairo, Egypt.

7

#7. Mother and Two Sisters: 10in (25cm) mother; 5in (13cm) sisters; coarse cotton cloth; 1982. The sequins are out of proportion for the dolls, but the total effect expresses the timelessness and hope of the people along the Nile. These primitive dolls are examples of the dolls capturing the attention of collectors today. They hold special memories for the authors of two small girls patiently waiting along a hot sand road for tourist buses.
MARKS: None.

#8. Lady Water Carrier: 15in (38cm); all painted wood; blue and white dress and headdress; wooden multi-colored striped water jug; stylized artist doll with a careful balance feature; 1982. This very modern Egyptian doll portrays a village woman as she makes her daily walk to the river for water. This type of factory-made doll can be found in other Middle East countries in various forms. Temple of Karnak in background.
MARKS: None.

8

#9. ***LEFT to RIGHT:*** **Cotton Picker***:* 8in (20cm); all cloth; lovely hand painted face; long black hair; green polka dot tunic and matching harem pants; red shoes with upturned toes; balances a bale of cotton on her head; 1982. **MARKS:** "Egyptian Doll///Onnig of Cairo//Onnig Alexanian//Egyptian Museum//Cairo, Egypt" on gold tag at waist which can be seen in the picture. **Carved Stone Statue:** 9in (23cm); all hand carved. **MARKS:** None.

9

#10. Double-Faced Egyptian Woman Muslim Doll: 8in (20cm); papier mâché head; cloth body; face on one side is very beautiful with Kohl-type black makeup and beautiful painted flesh tone on face; blue and gold necklace; large gold pendant earrings with inscribed Egyptian face; gold beads hang from pendant; black purdah-type half-veil and cloak; orange burlap body; white and yellow print dress; face on back of doll has no makeup but is nicely molded; veil covers entire face. This is a very unusual doll. *Sandy Strater Collection.*
MARKS: None.

10

11

#11. ***LEFT to RIGHT:*** **Mummy:** 9in (23cm); carved from wood which is scarce in dry Egypt. Although the head looks out of proportion, it is actually a wonderful likeness of Amenhotep IV (1365-1347 B.C.). He was the first Pharaoh to worship one god (the sun god Aten) and insist his subjects do the same. He even changed his name to Akhenaten. His wife was Nefertiti, and his son was Tutankhamun. A tiny wooden mummy is inside the mummy case. **MARKS:** None.

Mummy: 5.5in (14cm); intricately carved stone case with detailed carved wooden mummy inside. **MARKS:** None.

12

#12. ***LEFT to RIGHT:*** **Nesting Doll:** Painted with the design that decorates the lid of Nes-mut-neru's sarcophagus. **Mummy of Nes-mut-neru:** dating to 700-675 B.C. The lady was the wife of a priest of the Theban god Montu. The objects in her tomb were typical of Theban aristocracy of this period. The original mummy is in the Boston's Museum of Fine Arts Collection. **The Smallest Doll:** Shows the image of the mummy that survived over 3,000 years due to the advanced techniques of Egyptian burial. **Nesting Doll:** The largest mummy has the design of Nes-mut-neru's wooden outer sarcophagus.

MARKS: "Nesting Mummies" on box.

Background Wall Hanging from Judd Collection: (Left) *Osiris*, the ruler of the dead. (Right) *Re*, the sun God or creator of the earth.

#13. Shawabti (Ushabti): 10in (25cm); one piece limestone statue representing the scribe *Ramose*. The inscription on the horizontal strip says, "Ramose's face is painted dark ochre, illuminated by two big eyes with black and white details. The wig covering the ears has long cascading curls. The bare feet suggest the costume of the living. The headband opens out in the middle of the forehead in a blue lotus. A broad collar is indicated by red bands on a yellow background." The statue was purchased July 25, 1986 at Expo 86 in Vancouver B.C. Canada. *Sherry Morgan Collection.*
MARKS: See inscription explanation above.

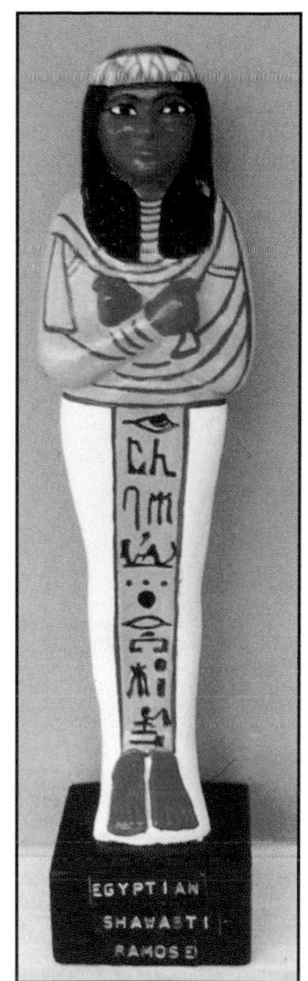

13

14

#14. ***LEFT to RIGHT:*** **Egyptian Couple and Woman: Large Female:** 11in (28cm); thick, pink cotton stuffed body, arms, legs; plaster head painted skin color; small bit of glued-on hair which shows under the black shawl over her head with gold circle decorations at the bottom; shawl is tied at the neck with a piece of blue cloth decorated with pink wool bows; heavy, long, turquoise cotton dress; at chest level hangs a black rectangle of cloth decorated with small metallic birds; stiffened cotton shoes. **Small Female:** 9.5in (24cm); cloth stuffed body; painted face; black gauze shawl over head, shoulder and skirt; white and green polka dot long cotton dress; hanging gilt earrings and snake wrist bands; yellow bead necklace with gold coin at end; faux leather slipper shoes. Following an Arab tradition, she wears a special lace covering over her face called a "haik" to prevent men from seeing her face. **Male Arab:** 11in (28cm); same body as large female; plaster head painted skin color; painted black hair; blue eyes; pink open/closed mouth; wears the traditional Arab "jalabiyah" of heavy cotton with brown vertical stripes which looks like a long nightgown; brocade collar and neck inset; stiffened cotton shoes; beige cotton cap. *Sherry Morgan Collection.*
MARKS: "1070 in Luxor" (a city in Egypt)

ETHIOPIA

Like other African countries, Ethiopia has many tribes and religions. The costumes depend on the climate and the religion. City inhabitants wear more decorative clothes than those in the primitive areas, especially in the warmer southern regions.

The "shamma"* is a long length of material wound around the body on top of other clothing. The way the shamma is draped tells the wearer's region. Women wear the shamma over dresses. The men wear it over pants and possibly a shirt. An example is shown below, although people often wear a much longer embroidered shamma than this one.

The usual costume is white, but today some wear a white dress with a patterned border, or possibly dresses of many different colors. Most of the clothes are made of cotton.

Jewelry – colored beads, ivory, necklaces made from the hair and tails of giraffes are worn, especially in the south. Silver and gold jewelry are worn by the more affluent. Christians wear a colored band around the neck called a "matab" and some wear Coptic crosses.

Some Ethiopians wear white turbans, high and round in shape. The monks have yellow ones.

*This is sometimes spelled "shama".

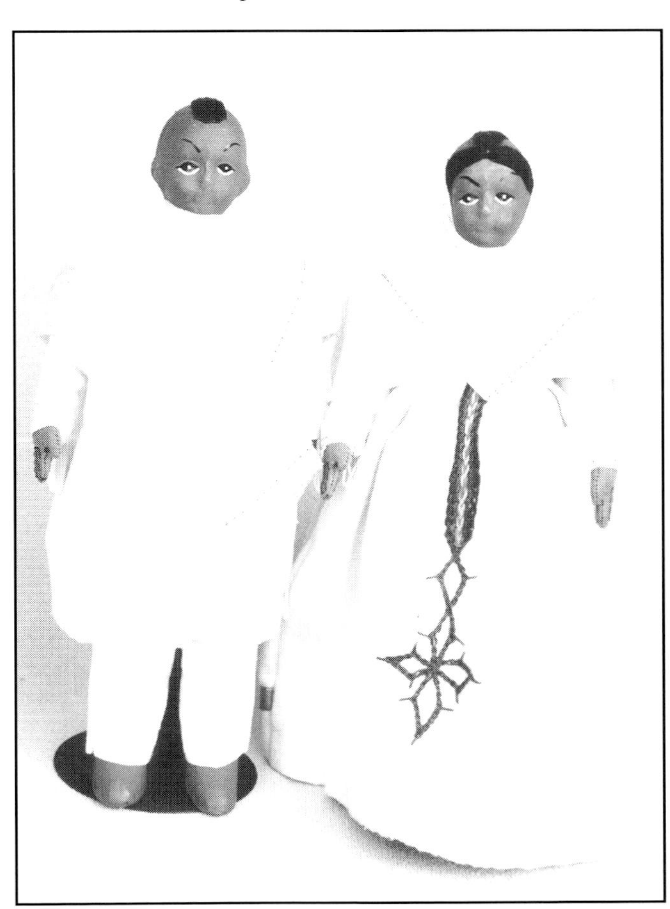

#15. Man and Woman from Church of the Holy Family, Addis Abba, Ethiopia: Man 9.75in (25cm); Woman 9.5in (24cm); burlap-type cloth body; papier mâché heads; wooden feet.
Coptic Christian Man wears white tunic with yellow stitching; split at sides; matching white pants; white net shawl covers half the body in front and back; thread hair in a middle strip in the center of the head.
Coptic Christian Woman wears a white flannel long dress with blue, red, yellow embroidery down the front; white net scarf, shorter in front than the man's, but longer in back; scarf covers her head; thread hair in form of cross on her head, and the rest of the head is bare under the veil. Purchased in Ethiopia, July, 1964.
MARKS: None on doll.

15

GHANA

Ghana, in western Africa, borders the Ivory Coast in the west, Burkina Faso in the north, Togo in the east, and the Gulf of Guinea on the south. It is a tropical country just north of the equator with a hot and damp climate.

Ghana may be more familiar to the reader as the Gold Coast, but changed its name when it became independent in 1957. Accra, a city of almost one million people, is its capital.

Wildlife is disappearing now that the land is being used for homes or farming. Ghana has set aside large pieces of land for national parks where animals such as lemurs, giraffes, hippopotamuses, buffalos, crocodiles, snakes, monkeys, antelopes, wild hogs, and birds can still be seen.

Many Ghanians wear Western-style clothing, but some men still wear long robes called ntamas. Some women wear ntamas as skirts with blouses called kababas. Most of the people are Muslims. Others are Christians.

Their arts and crafts include wood and ivory carving. A tropical rain forest in west central Ghana provides mahogany, ebony, and other valuable trees for lumber and carving Ghanian art. The Ashanti carve stools and beautiful statues. Other tribes carve wooden masks for use in ceremonies. Hand woven "kente" cloth is Ghana's most famous product. The bright colors and patterns are woven by Ashanti men.

#16. Ashanti Fertility Doll: 12in (31cm); one piece of wood; painted all black; round flat face with high forehead; carved eyebrows, eyes, nose, small lips; long neck; small horizontal carved arms, penis, legs, feet, and toes; incised on midriff is a square of slanted lines. This doll, called an "Akuba", is carved by a woman who hopes to have a beautiful child. 1992. *Sherry Morgan Collection.* **MARKS:** "Trade Aid Co." on paper which came with doll.

16

17

#17. Male and Female Ashanti Fertility Dolls: Male is 13in (33cm); Female is 11.5in (29cm); carved of local wood, shoe polish was used as paint, rubbed into the wood until it would not come off to the touch; female wears earrings and beaded belt, minimum clothing carved into figure; male also has some carved clothing; carving focus is on the face and intricate hair style. The dolls were sent to this country by a missionary of the World Council of Churches in 1966. Along with the dolls came this explanation.

"The doll was usually carved by the prospective father. If he wanted a boy, he carved a male, and if he wanted a girl, he carved a female. After the child was born, it was given to the child as a toy." *Carlton Brown Collection.* **MARKS:** None.

18

#18. Ashanti Fertility doll: 13in (33cm); one piece of carved wood painted all black; dressed in yellow top and matching skirt with typical design in red and black stripes and swirl; beads hanging down from head; necklace; bracelet hanging from short arms. This is an unusual Ashanti doll because it is dressed.
MARKS: None.

#19. Lady Carrying a Baby on Her Back: 7.5in (19cm); all cloth; hand woven fabric costume; dark red, yellow, green, black strips on tunic; blue for part of yoke and one sleeve; vertical stripes on lower part of tunic; matching hat; white and black handbag; silver jewelry; unseen baby in a pouch made by wrapping dress, on back. *Jackie Dukes Collection.*
MARKS: "Hand Made// in Ghana//E A A"

19

IVORY COAST *(For listing see page 22.)*

KENYA

Kenya is located north of Mt. Kilimanjaro and borders, Tanzania, Uganda, Sudan Ethiopa, Somali Republic, and the Indian Ocean. Today most of Kenya's 20 million people are agriculturalists. The rest are herders, hunters, fishermen or city dwellers. The tribal cultures include the Masai, Nilotic, Cushitic, Bantu, and Samburu.

In 1963, after a history of Portuguese, Arab, and British rule, Kenya gained her independence.

The Kenyans do take pride in their handmade artifacts, and the authors found that it was easier to find Kenyan statues (doll forms) than ones from many of the other African countries. There also was a greater variety because there are so many different tribes.

#20. Kenyan Doll: 10in (25cm); wooden head; sisal body and hair; collected in 1979. *Rosalie Whyel Museum of Doll Art. Susan Hedrick Photographer.*
MARKS: None.

20

#21. Banana Leaf Doll: 7in (18cm); dried banana leaves wrapped tightly; imitation leather blue dress; seed beads decorate face, head and collar of dress; from the middle of her dress hangs round plastic pink and red beads with cut cowrie shells; yellow plastic round beads decorate the ankles of her large feet; wire arm band on upper arms; purchased 1969 in Nairobi. *Sherry Morgan Collection.*
MARKS: None.

21

22

#22. Double Dolls of the Samburu Tribe in Northern Kenya: 5.5in (14cm); molded brown clay; man and woman joined together by clothes; both faces have sculpted eyes and mouths; noses with pierced nostrils and ears; short arms with indented lines for fingers; feet have indented toe lines; both are covered with a cloth skirt held on by a strip of cloth at their waists. The woman has black hair and charcoal-colored collar; her pierced ears have strings of glass beads; her face and chest are ocher colored (a native pigment). The man has a plastic ornament on his head; green wire extends from his forehead and white glass beads are embedded about his ears; long neck is ocher colored. Purchased at the African Pavilion, Canada World's Fair in Vancouver; 1986. *Sherry Morgan Collection.*
MARKS: "Made in Kenya" tag at the bottom of the doll.
The dolls in the left hand corner of the picture are another version of the same type of dolls.

23

#23. ***LEFT to RIGHT:*** **Boy:** 7.75in (20cm); hand carved; wire around neck; spring earrings; straw skirt; carved skirt underneath straw; late 1960s. **Warrior:** 8.5in (22cm); hand carved mahogany wood; wire around neck to extend neck upward; spring earrings; green cotton skirt; painted cardboard shield.

The jewelry around the neck determines the wealth of the owner.
MARKS: "Hand Carved//Made in Kenya" label on back.

#24. Masai Female Doll: 11.25in (29cm); carved from one piece of dark brown wood; white bead eyes; slit for mouth; carved hair; rings of multi-colored glass beads through her pierced ears; seed beads strung on wire around the neck and chest; arms decorated with silver wire; mitt hands with incised finger marks; magenta felt cloth dress sewn tight to body; two rings of glass beads around her ankles; carved 1.5in (4cm) base; carved pointed breasts with two strings of beads between them; 1969. Made by a member of the Masai tribe. *Sherry Morgan Collection.* **MARKS:** "1969 in the Amboseli Game Park in Kenya" on bottom of base.

24

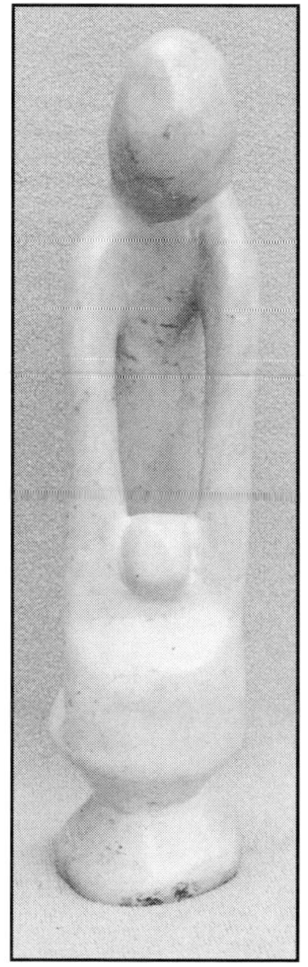

25

#25. Kenyan Natural Kisii Stone Mother and Child: 7.5in (19cm); 1990s. This famous sculpture was selected by the United Nations to represent the International year of the Child. The arms of the mother reach down while the arms of the child reach up to form a single warm embrace. Made of Kenyan Kisii stone, the piece is entirely worked by hand. The final form was highly polished with shark-skin and fish scales to give the stone its distinctive satin smooth feel. **MARKS:** "Specially hand-made in Kenya for Brimful House" tag on bottom of base.

26

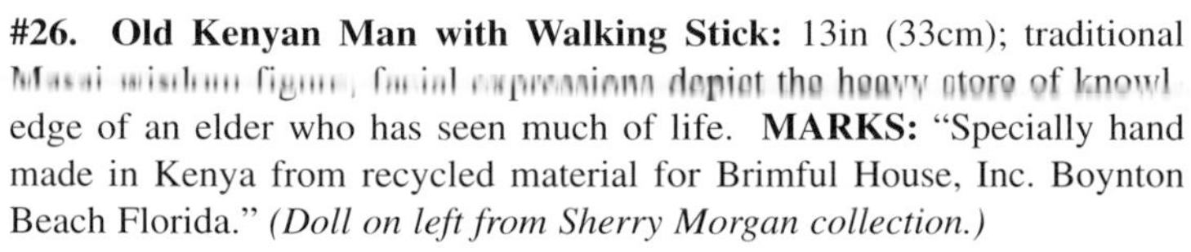

#26. Old Kenyan Man with Walking Stick: 13in (33cm); traditional Masai wisdom figure; facial expressions depict the heavy store of knowledge of an elder who has seen much of life. **MARKS:** "Specially hand made in Kenya from recycled material for Brimful House, Inc. Boynton Beach Florida." *(Doll on left from Sherry Morgan collection.)*

27

#27. Young Girl: 12in (31cm); beautifully carved; black painted cap on head; early 1970s. *Carlton Brown Collection.* **MARKS:** None.

#28. Kenyan Woman: 14in (36cm); carved wood; fertility pregnant doll; leather loin cloth with bead and shell trim; hemp hair; wire coil with 21 rings around her neck; black and red beads below wires; 1980s.The Kenyan girls add rings over a period of time, 21 is the correct number for an adult woman. This doll was purchased right on the equator. *Shirley Karaba Collection.* **MARKS:** None.

28

29

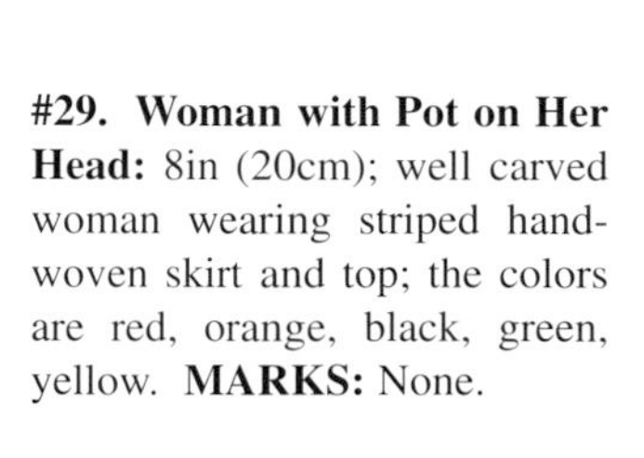

#29. Woman with Pot on Her Head: 8in (20cm); well carved woman wearing striped hand-woven skirt and top; the colors are red, orange, black, green, yellow. **MARKS:** None.

LESOTHO

Until 1966, Lesotho was the British colony of Basutoland. Entirely surrounded by the Republic of South Africa, Lesotho is a land of mountains, a high plateau, and a narrow lowland area. With limited agricultural resources and little industry, it is dependent upon South Africa for employment and manufactured goods.

The country is densely populated, and unlike some other African countries, it is an ethnically homogeneous country with the Basuto tribal group comprising over 90% of the population. The white population and other non-Basutos are prohibited from owning land.

Although Lesotho faces governmental and employment problems, it continues to make exquisite handicrafts as it did a century ago.

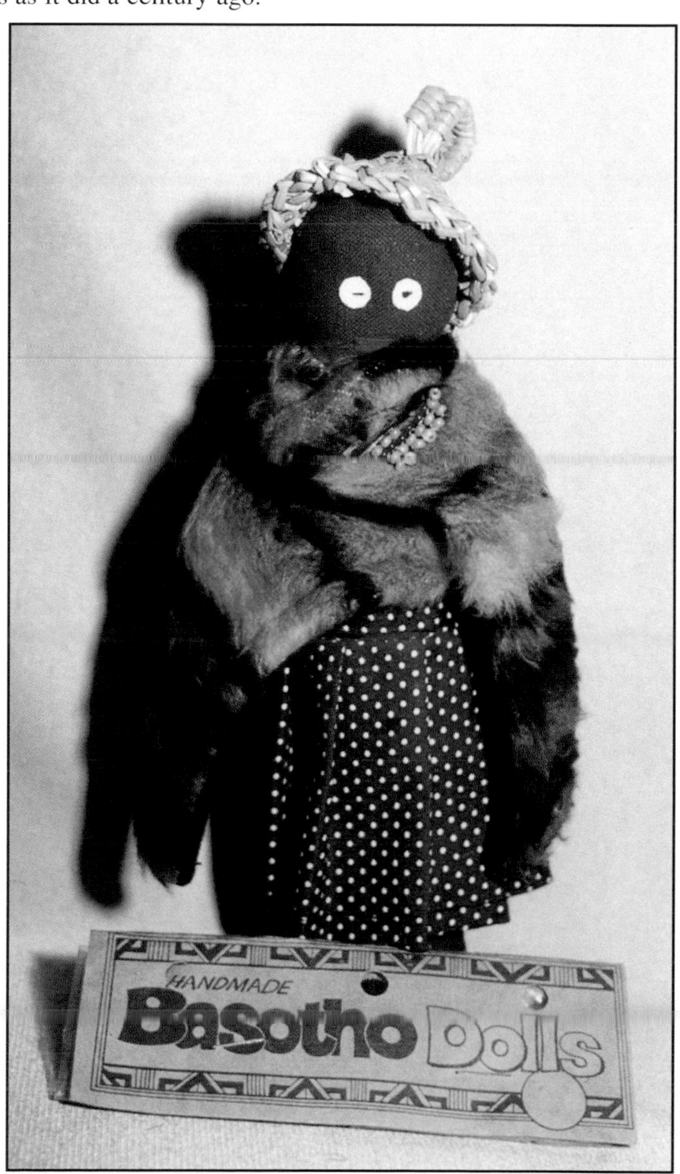

#30. Lesotho Doll: 9in (23cm); all dark cloth; button-type eyes; red felt mouth; woven straw head-piece: polka dot dress with blanket-type cape; 1981. This doll was purchased through SERRV. *Thelma Purvis Collection.*
MARKS: "Hand made Lesotho Dolls"

30

IVORY COAST

Prince Henry the Navigator, who sent ships to explore the riches and new route of the Far East, first heard of the Ivory Coast in 1495.

This land on the Gulf of Guinea is heavily forested and was a home for elephants and a source of ivory. There are several inhabiting tribes including the Agnis-Ashanti, Kroumen, Mande, and Baule. It was a center of trade for many years. In 1842, the French set up a permanent trading post, and by 1889, it was a French protectorate. Missionaries followed, but most of the people held to their traditional animist religions. The country became independent in 1960.

#31. ***LEFT to RIGHT*:** **YaKuba Tribe :** 14.5in (37cm); wood body, head, limbs with jointed shoulders; wood mask (Yakuba We mask); large painted eyebrows in dot form; carved and painted white slits for eyes; carved nose; red carved and painted protruding lips; headdress consists of a scarf around the head and neck with a woven blue and white headband, red wool fringe hanging from the ears and white hemp on a carved pointed hat; woven navy blue shirt with yellow, orange, and white stripes; hands hold white hemp for decoration; straw woven skirt; painted, decorated wood legs; feet covered with hemp. **MARKS:** "November, 1991" on bottom of stand. **Colonial Doctor:** 11.5in (29cm); carved wood; white helmet, shirt and shorts; black carved and painted stethoscope, shoes, and base; brown painted face and limbs; black painted eyebrows and pupils of eyes; carved pointed nose and full lips; large ears; white painted socks; 1994.
MARKS: None.
Sherry Morgan Collection.

31

LIBYA

Libya, the fourth largest country in Africa, is located in the north on the Mediterranean Sea. Most of the land is a desert, but it is rich in oil. It has a Mediterranean climate and enough rain in the winter to raise grain. 90% of the population lives in the coastal areas. Because of the oil revenues, it is a modern nation.

About 90% of the people are Arabic-speaking with Arab-Berber ancestry. The Berbers live in small isolated villages in the west. The predominate religion is the Sunni branch of Islam. The official language is Arabic.

#32. ***LEFT to RIGHT:*** **Tripoli Woman Carrying Water Jug on Shoulder:** 9.5in (24cm); blue and white, long print caftan with ruffle at bottom; black cape; tan scarf with black trim; 1970s. **Tripoli Dancing Couple:** 9.5in (24cm); baked clay heads; cloth over armature body; man dressed in gray "fez-like" hat with wide white band; red shirt; black pants; red shoes; woman dressed in white caftan with red sash and headscarf; red shoes; 1970s. **MARKS:** "Hand Made In Tripoli" on base of dancing couple; no marks on lady carrying water jar.
Thelma Purvis Collection.

32

MADAGASCAR

Madagascar is one of the world's largest islands. It is 250 miles off the coast of southeast Africa. As with many of the African counties, there has been much mixing of tribes and ethnic groups with their own customs and religions. The official languages are French and Malagasy.

It became an independent nation in 1960, but not without a series of problems.

Agriculture is the main occupation in these islands. Rice and cassava are leading subsistence crops. Coffee is the principal export crop, and Madagascar is the world's leading producer of cloves and vanilla.

#33. ***LEFT to RIGHT:*** **Elephant:** Carved ebony elephant; ivory tusks, toes, eyes; 6.5in (17cm) long; 6in (15cm) long; late 1800s. *Hugh H. Wikle Collection.* **MARKS:** None. **Madagascar Man Carrying Ducks to Market***:* 5.5in (14cm); painted carved wood head; cloth over wire frame body; white print suit with high neck; yellow, orange, beige print slim pants; orange baskets with ducks balanced on pole; 1960s. **MARKS:** "Madagascar" printed on base. **Lady with Baby Carried on her back:** 6in (15cm); painted carved wood heads, arms, legs; black, orange, purple print dress; white shawl wrapped around her shoulders and tightly tied so baby will not fall; carries a pink basket with rice on her head. **MARKS:** "Madagascar" printed on base.

33

MALAWI

Malawi is a beautiful country in southeast Africa. Lake Nyasa, covers almost one-third of this narrow country. Much of the land is forested. The country lies in the Great Rift Valley, but has highlands and plateaus from 2000 to 8000 feet high and mountains to 10,000 feet high. The climate is warm in the valley and comfortable in the highlands.

Lilongwe, the capital is a small, beautiful city. The doll in the picture comes from Blantyre, further south. This city bears the name of the explorer Livingston's birthplace in Scotland.

This land became self-governing in 1963, and took the name of Malawi in April, 1964. It became a member of the United Nations in December, 1964.

34

#34. Small Angoni Warrior of the Bantu Race: 5in (13cm); dark brown hard plastic body; headdress is swirl of real lion's main; his skirt is made of furry lion hide; holds a spear; small multi-colored beads decorate the neck, wrists; subtribe of the Zulu; 1960s-1970s. **MARKS:** "Serrv//Malawi" on bottom of foot.

MOROCCO

The souks are the centers of native trade in the Moroccan cities. With stalls selling almost anything needed or wanted by Moroccan citizens (See *page 27 middle*) and entertainment in the form of magicians, monkey trainers, and snake charmers. In the evening the girls line up in a circle near the center of the crowd and dance the *ahouache* as the tambourines and drums beat out a strong rhythm.

Morocco is a land of many differences. The Sahara desert is on the southern boundary, the Mediterranean Sea is on the north. In between there is rich farm land and modern cities. Fashions include modern business suits for men, although they may wear a loose fitting robe called a *djellaba* to protect their suits. There are Paris fashions for the ladies, but the authors have seen them don the long robes and veils over their Paris fashions when they enter the Casbah and take them off again as they come into the modern area of the cities. Muslim men still wear the traditional Muslim caftans and fez full time, and some women may wear the robes and veils from head to foot when they are not in their homes.

The water sellers wear colorful traditional clothes of their area, tribe, or religion *(see below and page 28 bottom).*

On the edge of the Sahara live the Blue men and women. The hair, skin, and beards of these nomads have turned blue because of the indigo-colored dyes used in their clothes.

Although some women still wear the veil in public, women are important. There is a Moroccan saying, "The man rules the family, but the women rule the man." Women have professional and governmental jobs, and they have the right to vote. Morocco is a very cosmopolitan country.

#35. Moroccan Water Carrier*:* 6in (15cm); all-leather body; white cotton shirt; red cotton tunic; black simulated metal shoulder guards and armor in front and on sides decorated with beads and metal decoration; carries a leather water bag and cup on left side of gold chain attached to collar of armor; metal bell is attached to chain on right side; high turban decorated with heavy brown thread; dhoti pants; leather sandals; 1960s.
MARKS: None.

35

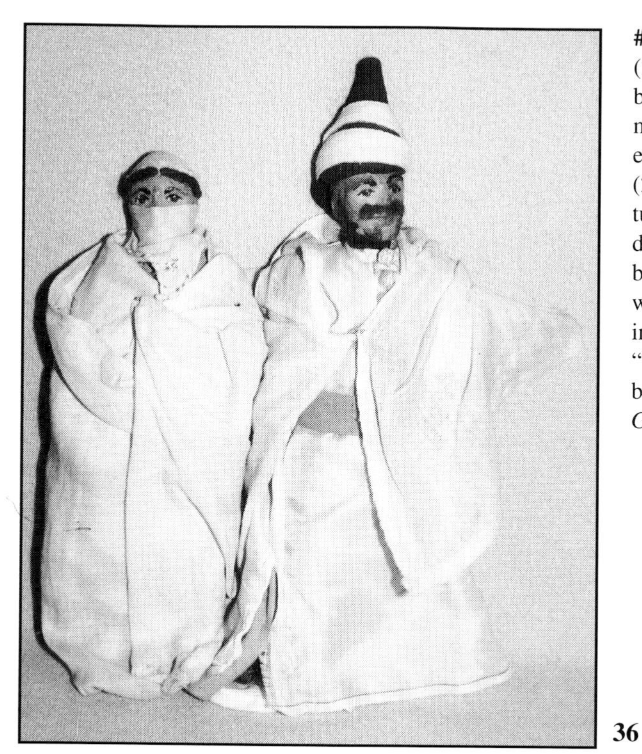

36

#36. ***LEFT to RIGHT:*** **Woman:** 8in (20cm); papier mâché head and body; blue kafton under white Purdah garments; mask trimmed with blue embroidery; 1952. **Man:** 9.5in (24cm); red felt conical fez with white turban material wound around the border; blue thawab trimmed with woolen balls unseen under chiffon thawab; white linen djellaba to protect clothing; white leather shoes. **MARKS:** "Tangiers, 1952" on soles of shoes of both man and woman.
Gigi Williams Collection.

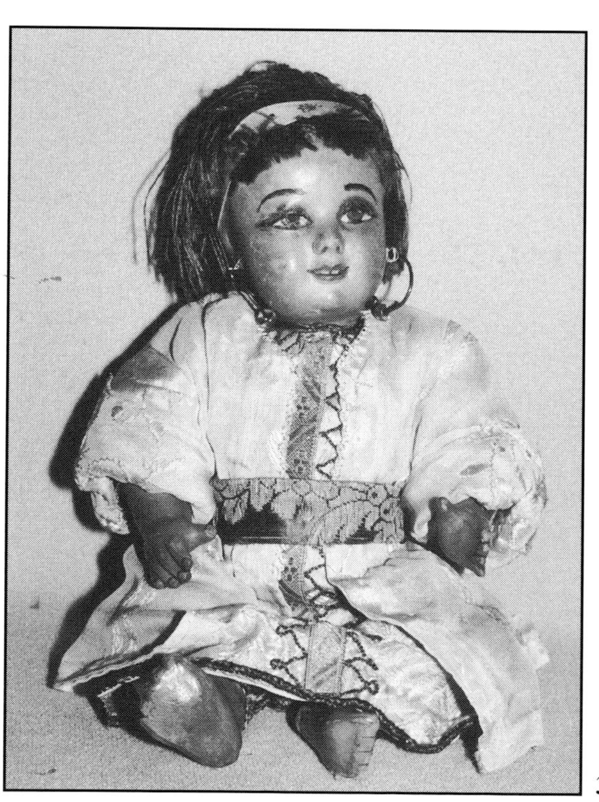

37

#37. Moroccan Baby: 12in (31cm); all leather bent-leg baby; auburn floss hair; jointed open/closed mouth with inset teeth; coarse petticoat; cream damask tunic with maroon and black braid; green ribbon trim; silk pants and headband; hoop earrings; made in leather bazaar in Tangiers; imported by Kimport in 1945. *Shirley Karaba Collection.* **MARKS:** None.

#38. Saudie Peddler from French Morocco: 9.5in (24cm); all leather doll; painted leather face; beige boucle robe; hooded desert royal blue djellaba to protect his orange cotton robe and pants robe from the sand; leather sandals; carries bolt of red cloth. *Beverly Findlay Collection.*
MARKS: "Saudi Man//French Morocco".

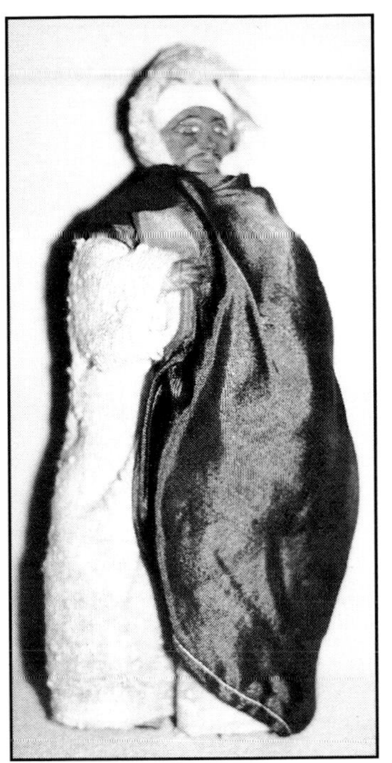

38

39

#39. ***LEFT to RIGHT:*** **Wife:** 8in (20cm); all leather; dressed in the traditional robes of the Saharra people (Muslim). **Business Man:** 9in (20cm); all leather; dressed in the traditional men's attire of the Sahara desert residents.
MARKS: None on dolls.

#40. ***LEFT to RIGHT:*** **Boy with Musical Instrument:** 4.5in (12cm); painted carved wood; brown tunic with yellow trim; red pants; high black shoes; round flat turban with circles painted on top; gold instrument; 1966. **MARKS:** "Marrakech" seal on base. **Clothing Street Merchant:** 7.5in (19cm) all carved, painted wood; man's green costume decorated with black and yellow stripes; red and yellow fez; yellow and red stockings; black shoes; stands on base; 1966.
MARKS: None.

40

41

#41. Woman from Rabat with Baby: 9in (23cm); all leather doll and baby; painted faces on each doll; multi-colored straw hat over cotton head shawl on woman; head-shawl on baby; red, green and white flowered blouse and red and white striped skirt on woman; leather shoes with turned-up toes; 1964.
This is a well-made leather doll and baby.
MARKS: None on doll.

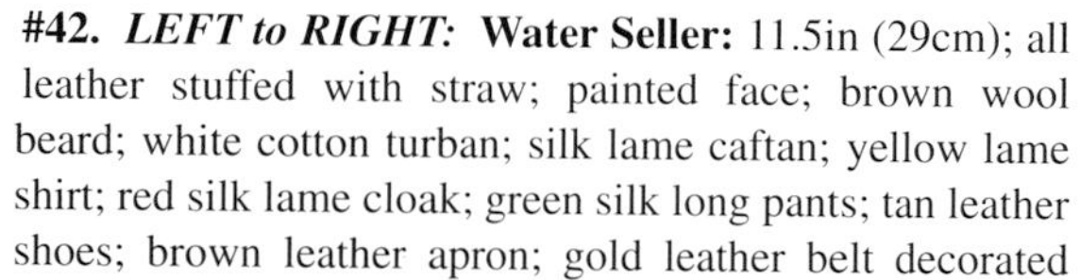

#42. ***LEFT to RIGHT:*** **Water Seller:** 11.5in (29cm); all leather stuffed with straw; painted face; brown wool beard; white cotton turban; silk lame caftan; yellow lame shirt; red silk lame cloak; green silk long pants; tan leather shoes; brown leather apron; gold leather belt decorated with sequins and beads; carries a brown leather water bag. Attached to his apron straps are drinking cups. A silver bell is attached at the end of the chain to let everyone know he is coming; 1934. **MARKS:** None.
Man on Camel: 9.5in (24cm); leather hand-stitched body; painted face; white cotton turban with black wool to hold it on; attached to camel with gold tacks; holds onto reins of the camel with both hands; 1987. **MARKS:** None.
Sherry Morgan Collection.

42

NATAL

#43. Lady Stirring Food for a Meal: 5in (13cm); celluloid doll; black mohair; white blouse with printed red roses; pink skirt with white leaf design; white sandals; carved wooden food preparation center; 1950-60. **MARKS:** "Natal" woodburned on base.

NAMIBIA

Namibia is in the southwest corner of Africa. It borders South Africa, Botswana, Angola, Zambia, and the Atlantic Ocean. It is a land of sand, dunes, disappearing streams, and lakes. Much of the eastern part of the country is the Great Kalahari desert which is almost barren of life. The country used to be called South West Africa.

There is a central plateau which has a pleasant climate, but along the coast the damp fog comes every morning, and as it meets the desert, it quickly evaporates and becomes very hot. Nights are cold.

African tribes have lived in Namibia when other parts of Africa were uninhabited. First the San and the Khoikhoi peoples came and left rock drawings preserved by the climate. The Damara group inhabitants were there when the Herero migrated from the east looking for better grazing land.

Missionaries came at the end of the 19th century, and finally the country became a colony of Germany. Like other Africans, the people of Namibia fought long and hard for freedom which was finally attained in the 1990 tribe unification.

44

#44. Herero Lady with Victorian-style Dress: 8in (20cm); all cloth doll; beautiful orange, green, maroon, black and white print dress and matching headdress, shawl and apron; real crystal earrings; 1993. *Jackie Dukes Collection.* **MARKS:** None.

NIGERIA

Nigeria is on the west coast of Africa on the Gulf of Guinea. With twice the land area of California, it starts at the coast with a swamp, forest belt, a tropical rain forest, and then climbs to a cooler plateau of 2000-4000 feet. Finally the border approaches the Sahara Desert.

There are about 250 different tribes with their own customs and languages. The Hausa are Muslims, tall and elegant. The Ibo or Ekpe live in villages built in forest clearings in the south. Benin is a city state in the south well known for their bronze sculptures. (*See page 7*). Some of the natives carve excellent wood thornwood figures.

Before the spread of Christianity, twin births were feared by some tribes and celebrated by others such as the Yorube Tribe who had two dolls, carved to represent the children. If one child died, the surviving child carried the doll on his back, the same way a Yoruba mother carried her child. This custom of creating *Ibeji* dolls has died.

The authors bought their first figures in an Art Museum gift shop. They can also be found in import stores or from the Brimful House, Inc. in Boynton Beach, Florida.

45

#45. ***LEFT to RIGHT:*** **Nigerian Carved Thornwood Classroom:** 3.5in (9cm) by 7in (13cm) by 8in (20cm); schoolroom scene with eight students, each face with a different expression. The teacher is at the board which has the letters A-I on it. A desk with books and a pencil and a chair for the teacher is on the left. 1990s. *Brimful House, Boynton Beach, Florida.* **MARKS:** "Thornwood classroom scenes (Made from recycled materials); Hand Made in Nigeria for Brimful House" on bottom of base. **Thornwood Two Men Playing Basketball:** 5in (13cm) by 4.5in (12cm) by 2in (5cm); Two carved thornwood Nigerian boys playing basketball; 1990s. **MARKS:** "Thornwood Two Men Playing Basket Ball; hand made in Nigeria for Brimfield House" on bottom of base.

46

#46. Thornwood Canoe with Three Men: 9in (23cm) long; hand carved; two men with smaller hats are paddling; man in middle with cone-shaped hat is probably the chief; he is not paddling; each man has different facial features; canoe is passing by a native village. *Background photography by Harriet Beerbas, Dollco.* **MARKS:** "Handmade in Nigeria for Brimful House, Boynton Beach, Florida" seal on bottom of canoe.

47

#47. Ekpe Mask Doll from the Efic Tribe of S.E. Nigeria: 14.5in (37cm); brown knitted wool body and limbs over rolled paper; tuft of red dyed plant fiber on top of head; feet made from heavy pipe cleaner wire; wrists and ankles have dyed red, purple and natural color twisted fiber wreaths around them; at neck is a very large and full wreath collar of the same color and fiber; at waist is a blue and pink cloth apron; Zimbabwe stamp was put on by the owner; 1994. The word Ekpe (pronounced Egbo) is a good luck symbol. A scared spirit, his face must be covered. *Sherry Morgan Collection.* **MARKS:** None.

SOUTH AFRICA

South Africa, the southernmost country in the world, divides two great oceans, the Atlantic and the Indian Ocean. In the Age of Exploration it was a necessary stopping point for boats from Europe to the Orient.

With four provinces: Cape of Good Hope; Orange Free State; Natal and Transvaal; and three capital cities: Cape Town, home of Parliament; Pretoria, home of government offices and Orange Free State, home of the national courts; South Africa is a country of rich resources and modern conveniences.

South Africa has a diverse population which includes the San or Bushmen, the Khoikhoi or Hottentots, the Zulus, and the English and Dutch. The Dutch, known as Afrikaners, are proud of their African heritage. Asians who have also lived here for centuries, wish to preserve the "old ways" as well.

The dolls shown in this section, for the most part, are examples of the art and culture of the African tribes. The Zulus, Xhose, Ndebele, Sotho, Tswanas, and Shangans are known for their beadwork dolls. These dolls, with their color coded messages, are highly collectible. The reader should be aware that American, English, French, German, etc. dolls of the present and past are also available. Many South American residents are doll collectors of antique, collectible, and modern dolls. There are also many modern doll artists who are creating excellent play dolls for children as well as art dolls for the collector (*see below*).

#48. Ruella Artist Doll from South Africa: 22.5in (57cm); wax over hand modeled black porcelain for shoulderhead, lower arms and hands, lower legs and feet; well defined brows, cheeks, lips, pierced ears with gold hoop earrings, feathered eyebrows; brown glass inserted paper-weight eyes; dimpled cheeks; light red painted, molded lips; eight inset teeth; brown curly acrylic wig; brown cloth body stuffed with cotton; upper arms wired; legs jointed to body with thread loops. Excellent color shading of the porcelain parts. She wears a navy blue flower print cotton dress used extensively by the native South Africans; white eyelet insert at chest; matching underskirt and pantalettes; handknitted yellow sweater with matching socks; handmade brown leather shoes; 1993. One-of-a-Kind created by Tranvaal doll artist Ruella Mossom. *Sherry Morgan Collection.*
MARKS: "1993" on back of doll.

48

49

#49. ***LEFT to RIGHT:*** **Blanket Lady:** 9in (23cm) heavily stuffed chocolate brown felt; glued facial features; beaded earrings; orange felt upper dress with beaded forms; white felt bottom; black felt ruffle around entire skirt; white beaded purse in left hand; (See Page 33 for list of tribes that used beads for making dolls). **MARKS:** "Blanket Lady in Transvaal//Zulu Africa//Xhosa Tribe" store tag from Higbee Company in Cleveland, Ohio. **Woman with Child:** 15in (38cm); heavily stuffed chocolate brown felt; sewn felt facial features bright colored and white bead costume. The child (Doek Doll) is made entirely of beads except for the inch long coils of wire to stretch her neck. The doll was made in the South African Red Cross Rehabilitation center, Durban. **MARKS:** None.

50

#50. Ndebele Tribal Doll: 11in (28cm); black stockinette over wood body; leatherette skirt; beaded apron; blanket-cape with bead trim; legs are stacked gold metal rings; beaded shoes; 1990. *Shirley Karaba Collection.* **MARKS:** None.

#51. Xhosa Baby of the Bantu Group: 4.5in (12cm); body all hard modeled clay; blanket with white painted triangular designs on edges; baby has molded hair; incised slits for eyes; snub nose with indented large nostrils; protruding round lips with indented closed mouth; molded body with indented navel; at neck is a leather flap with colored seed beads. Doll came in burlap bag; 1994. The tribe name is pronounced "Kosa." Purchased in George, South Africa. *Sherry Morgan Collection.* **MARKS and TAG:** "Tribal Africa//handmade pottery//Bantu Baby.

51

52

#52. Ndebele Woman: 11in (28cm); wood body; head covered in back with black cloth; covered in front with red beads; white beads (in flower pattern) used for eyes, nose, mouth; upper torso and short arms beaded in multiple colors; around neck and legs are rolled bands of cloth covered in beads; at waist is a rolled cloth band of green beads and yellow beaded flowers; lower torso in back is covered by black cloth with apron in a chevron design. 1993. Ndebele is pronounced "N du belly." Purchased in Capetown, South Africa at the Victoria and Albert Wharf. *Sherry Morgan Collection.*
MARKS: None.

#53. Bushman (San) Tribal Doll: 13in (33cm); sand and resin molded head, shoulderplate, lower arms and hands, lower legs and feet; molded resin hair, beard at chin, ears, and broad flat nose; pierced eyes; wrinkled and full wide, lined lips; molded fingers and toes; body made of brown leather and stuffed with pellets; wears tan leather karoso (loin cloth) decorated with two painted circular designs; leather short vest; at neck and knee are traditional white beads (originally these were made from ostrich shells); bamboo quiver for arrows on his right shoulder; wood bow on left shoulder; shoulders and knees jointed by sewing; he sits in a traditional two-piece wood chair with a carved elephant backing which was carved in Zimbabwe. Purchased in Capetown, South Africa in May, 1994 at the Victoria and Albert Pier. Made in a limited edition by Dawie Smit. *Sherry Morgan Collection.*
MARKS: None.

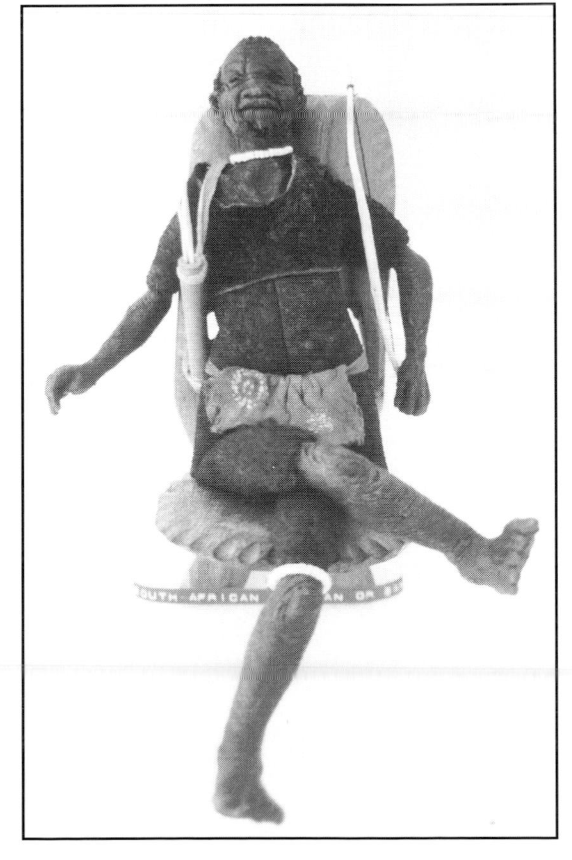

53

54

55

***LEFT:* #54. Ndebele Tribe Woman:** 15.5in (39cm); cloth stuffed head, body, short arms; wood legs and feet; legs wrapped in silver wire; square feet wrapped in black cloth decorated with seed beads; ankles have red seed decoration; two gold rings on neck which signify wealth; face totally beaded; blue headband; black and white beads for eyes and nose; head band uses white beads in an x-shape is decorated with red and white beads; black leather-like shirt; soft flannel blanket in bold blue, yellow, magenta rectangles over shoulder; multicolored beads around shoulders; 1994. Purchased in Cape Town at the Victoria and Albert Wharf. The doll is from the Transvaal Area. *Sherry Morgan Collection.*

***RIGHT:* #55. Cone Doll of Ndebele Tribe:** 20in (51cm); cone-shaped doll filled with straw; head covered in black cloth; cloth arms ending in round cloth balls; arms and chest covered in multi-colored seed beads; white seed bead nose and eyes with red bead center; white and blue beads act as a headband; long black wool hair stand decorated with intermittent colored beads in back; gold bands (made of copper) at neck represent wealth; two round cloth beaded balls represent breasts; four different colored bead necklaces encircle the red and green colored twine torso; bottom of patterned Kitengi shirt cloth; 1994. *Sherry Morgan Collection.* **MARKS:** None.

TANZANIA

Tanzania lives in the shadow of Mount Kilimanjaro in southeast Africa. Bordering Kenya, Rwanda Burundi, Zaire, Zambia, and the Indian Ocean, Tanzania was formerly the countries of Tanganyika and Zanzibar.

Many different tribes have inhabited Tanzania - the Sans, Bantue, Egyptians, and Arabs – each leaving their mark. The Bantu developed the government and farming economy of Tanzania. In the 1400s the Portugese, seeking a route to the East, started trading and taking slaves back to Europe. Germans colonized the area in 1885 followed by the English after World War II. Finally, in 1952 Tanzania became independent.

Today, Swahili and English are the two main languages. Swahili is based on Bantu, but it has many dialects. Two tribes, the Sandawe and Hadza speak a "click" language.

Their arts include folklore, dances, poetry, songs, musical instruments and wood carvings. The Masai produce elaborate masks, shields, and spears. The Makond people of Southern Tanzania and Northern Mozambique are famous for their ebony carvings. Their developed style, "shitana", is characterized by extremely exaggerated and detailed forms from ebony wood. The Makonde are considered by many to be the finest wood carvers in all of Africa because of the difficulty in working with the ebony medium. To the right is a Makonde carving.

#56. Tree of Life: 14.5in (37cm); figures carved into ebony wood called mpingo in East Africa after the sound an axe makes when it strikes the wood. Ebony is so hard, strong, and dense that in many respects it behaves more like metal than wood. The figures represent the *Mahoka*, friendly goodly spirits inhabiting the forest.The Mahoka, a strong, positive life force, protects and nurtures the animals, trees, and people who depend upon the forest for living. They are often depicted bearing food and gifts, hence the name "Tree of Life." 1990s. **MARKS:** "Tanzania//Brimful House, Boynton Beach, Florida" on underside of carving base.

56

57

#57. ***LEFT to RIGHT:*** **Tanzanian Carved Ebony Figures:**
Woman: 12.5in (32cm); elongated figure. **Skeleton Figure:** 14.5in (37cm); typical example of the elegant, exaggerated Shitani figures; these are also made in triple figures. **Woman and Man Tanzanian Carved Ebony Masai Heads:** 10.5in (27cm) tall. Regal herdsmen and warriors, the Masai roam the plains of East Africa much the same way they have for millennia. The statues are still carved in the old ways. *Brimful House, Inc.* **MARKS:** None.

TUNISIA

Tunisia is an African Arab country wedged between two larger neighbors, Algeria to the west and Libya to the east and the Mediterranean Sea and the Sahara, sea of sand.

A large diversity of peoples and cultures allows for many fashions. Some women wear the latest French fashions - sometimes hidden by a sifsari. Its loose folds can carry babies and packages, or it can be a veil, pulled in front of the wearers' mouth and held together by her teeth. Other poorer women wear regular Western clothes under their sifsari.

Another garment is the mellia, a loose drape-like sari worn in combination with another loose drape across the shoulders called the futa. This is pinned to the Melia by large silver pins.

Berber women wear black kohl makeup. Faces are often tattooed with ocher and blue dots *(see dolls on page 40)*. For special occasions designs are painted on hands. Jewelry is an important part of the costume because it represents the savings of the family.

Men often wear western business suits, adding a chehia on their head. This is a type of fez which may be brimless and tall, round or flattop. Usually it is in brown or red depending on the part of the country or area the man lives.

The traditional garment for men is the djellaba, a short sleeved tunic reaching to the ankles. A much longer, loose robe, a gandourah is worn in the desert. With its bat-winged, cowl-like hood, the gandourah provides protection from the sand, heat and cold.

Tunisia is an old civilized country making a transition to the modern world.

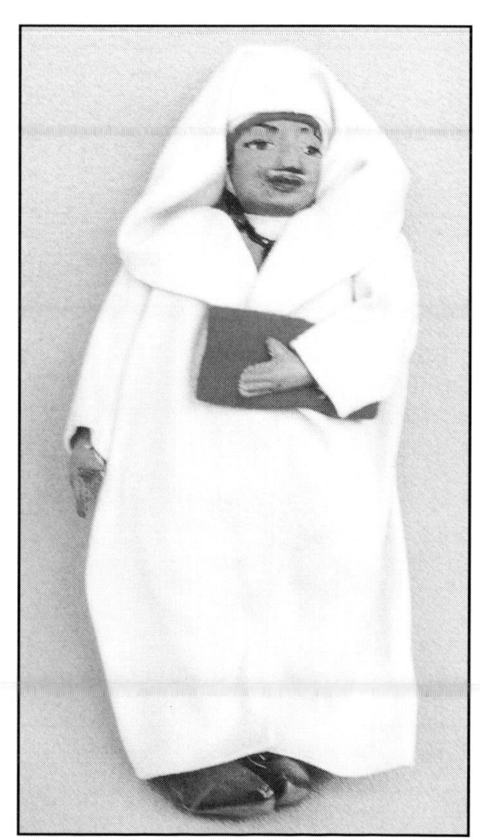

58

#58. Tunisian Holy Man: 8in (20cm); leather head, arms, legs; cotton body; real hair mustache; well-made cotton flowing robe called sthawab or sometimes kaftan with attached hood; white turban trimmed in red underneath the hood; gray shirt with blue braid underneath robe; white pants; red prayer shawl in his arms; blue suede, turned-up Arab-type shoes; 1959. A well-made Arab doll. **MARKS:** "Tunisia" on tag.

59

#59. Tunisian Girl: 10.5in (27cm); vinyl face and body; four kohl marks on face; black skirt with blue stripes around bottom, white top; purple headdress; black fringed shawl; tin ornaments on necklace; black rings around ankles; 1968. *Carlton Brown Collection.* **MARKS:** None.

#60. Arabic Girl: 7.5in (19cm); all hard plastic; sleep eyes; kohl marks around eyes; black cross on cheek, inverted "y" on chin; inner finger are stained red; blue hand-woven dress wrapped around her body and tied with wool yarn at waist; long shawl over head from same material as dress; gold chain ending in gold flowers decorates her headdress; blue beads on chest ending in silver pendant engraved with half moon and a star; thread wig; 1966. *Sherry Morgan Collection.* **MARKS:** None.

60

#61. Masked Figure: 10in (25cm); carved wood; braided bark strips support a cloth head mask on top of head; early 1950s. **MARKS:** None.

61

ZAIRE

Republic of Zaire, a part of the Congo, lies in a huge basin of forests, plains, mountains drained by the Congo River. A thriving nation, Zaire contains 200 or more tribes who speak as many as 400 different languages. Bantu and Pygmies are the largest tribes. They ornament their clothes and other art with beads. They are also wood carvers and sculpturers.

The southwest Congo people make statues studded with stones and nails. The Yaka people make masks and doll-like figurines. The people of the southern central area carve figures in traditional royal and ceremonial dress. The southeast natives make Madonna-like statues of mothers and children with brightly colored dresses that have a pouch for carrying babies and toddlers. All the tribes weave, make pottery, dance and sing according to the old customs.

Zaire is also the land of the Ituri Forest and the Pygmies - a small stature group, averaging 4.5 (139cm) feet. The Pygmies are more immune to tropical diseases than other Africans, and they are satisfied to hunt for a living and stay in the forest. They do not wear much clothing - often no more than a loincloth, but of course as in all societies, the young people are changing some of the old ways. Their arts include masks, figurines, weaving, pottery making, dancing and singing according to old customs. Almost every city and village in Zaire offers native handicrafts for sale to the general public and tourists.

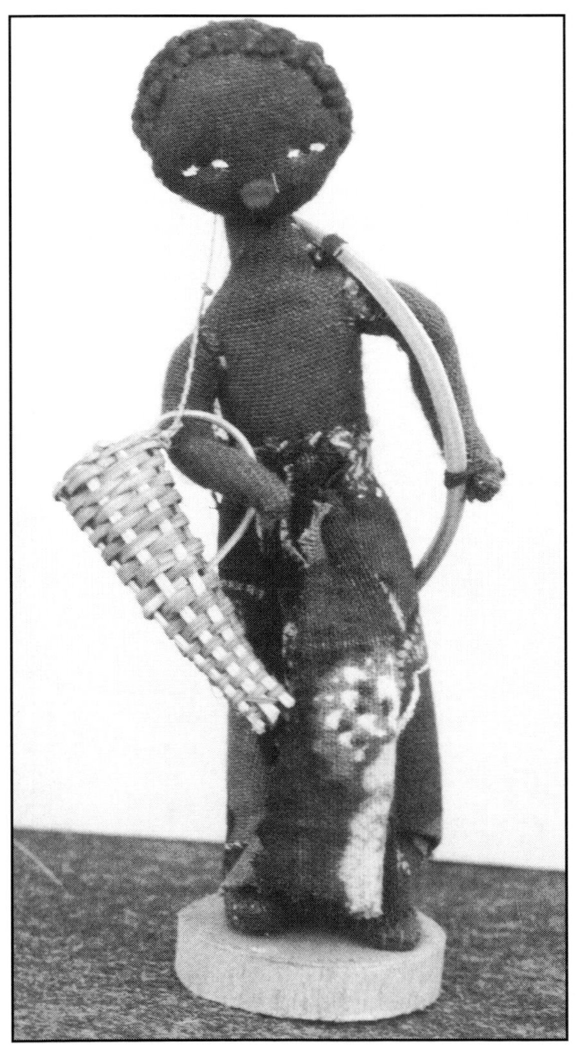

#62. Boy with Bow and Arrows: 6in (15cm); very primitive; all cloth; hand embroidered face; dark blue and yellow print skirt; 1970s. *Eleanor Niles Collection.* **MARKS:** None.

62

63

#63. Old Zairean Figure: 15in (38cm); old carved wood figures. The art work of many of the tribes of this part of Africa was made of wood. Over the years weather conditions caused deterioration, and since art was traditional, they just destroyed the old and made new. The Brimful House of Boynton Beach, Florida recently rediscovered a small group of wood figures over 90 years old. Each one is slightly different.
MARKS: None.

#64. Primitive Doll: 5.5in (14cm); knit material over wire armature; embroidered hair; white eyes; red felt lips; red toenails; reed fishing basket with one shoulder yoke; cotton wrap around skirt; 1970s. *Eleanor Niles Collection.* **MARKS:** None.

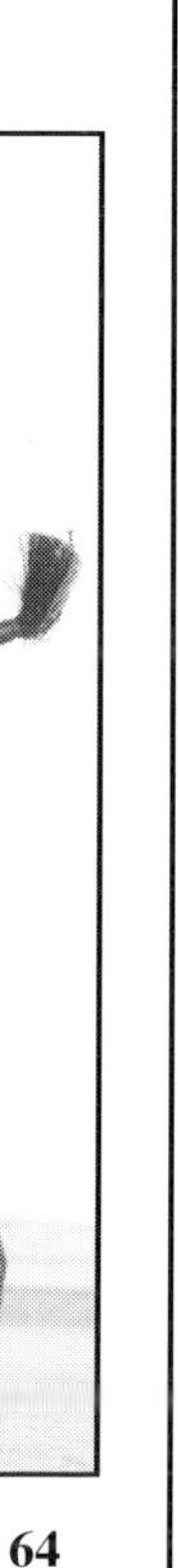

64

ZAMBIA

The Bantu people began migrating into South Africa about 2000 years ago. By the 7th century they were trading ivory, rhinoceros horns, copper, and slaves with other tribes. One of the countries they occupied is now known as Zambia.

Modern Zambian history started when Cecil Rhodes began to excavate minerals, and Europeans began to arrive to work the mines. Tensions between the Europeans and Africans increased. Land was taken from the natives and given to the Europeans until a group of natives formed the Northern Rhodesia African Mine Workers Union.

By 1958, the Zambian African National Congress was formed and elections took place. By 1964, Zambia was an independent country.

Most of Zambia is a high plateau covered by grassy savanna which is occupied by about 7 million people of the Lozi, Bemba, Luanda, and the Ngoni ethnic groups. Although most speak their native languages at home, English is the official language taught in schools.

65

#65. Zambia Girl: 3in (8cm); intricately carved from Zambian soapstone; zigzag skirt pattern; curly hair style; 1990s.
MARKS: "Made in Zambia//Brimful House Incorporated, Boynton Florida" seal on base.

ZANZIBAR

Zanzibar, an island off the coast of Tanzania, has been an important trading center between the Africans and Asians for centuries. Its population and buildings are a combination of Asian, Arab, and African influences. The most famous architecture is carved doors dating back to the 17th century. Tourists like to visit the island. The doll below is a coffee vendor waiting at the airport to welcome travelers.

#66. Coffee Vendor: 9.5in (24cm); baked clay face and shoulderplate; leather body and straw wrapped sturdy pole; fingers, legs and feet are wood wrapped in leather; white shirt; red, blue, and white plaid long skirt; tan vest with large pockets and white cotton binding; white quilted native hat; brass coffee pot which needs cleaning to bring back the shine; 1964. A well-made doll purchased at the Zanzibar Airport in July, 1964. **MARKS:** None on doll.

66

ZIMBABWE *(Old Rhodesia)*

It was not an easy shift of power in 1980 between the white colonials who have lived in Rhodesia for generations and the native tribes, including Asian and people of mixed ethnic origins, who have lived there for centuries. However, each side is trying to maintain both cultures peacefully for future generations to understand and enjoy. Today Zimbabwe is one of the most modern African countries.

The Black majority is blending into the new future and still trying to enjoy their rich culture of dances, music, crafts, and tradition. There is a Cultural Park where visitors can see the "old ways" in the comfort of new hotels. Stone sculptures from Zimbabwe have achieved international recognition and are eagerly sought by art collectors *(see below).* Other craft attractions include wood masks, basket weaving, carved wooden headrests, ornamented knives and gourds, musical instruments and dolls. A significant development in the preservation of tribal art began in the workshops of Harare's National Gallery during the 1960s.

With a moderate climate and rainy season, Zimbabwe is divided between a plain in the central section and highlands in the east. The famous Victoria Falls is there for both natives and visitors to enjoy.

While English is widespread, and taught in schools, the tribes are trying to maintain their own languages. The Shona and Ndebele are related to and speak a version of the Bantu language. In the 1800s some members of the Zulu tribe came here to escape problems in South Africa.

#67. Bahule (Guard): 9.5in (24cm); light, carved wood; two black painted and carved horns on top of head; carved triangle shapes in black and white around face; white slit eyes with black painted lids, eyebrows, nose; black mouth in round shape surrounded with white lips; white plant fiber nailed on for hair; tan woven fiber on body for clothing; hands carved to hips; feet carved into base; 1994. *Sherry Morgan Collection.*

MARKS: "Bahule//To protect friends from illness and evil spirits".

67

68

#68. ***LEFT to RIGHT:*** **Father, Mother, Teach Son to Dance:** *(Makishi Tribe):* **Father (Kalelina):** 13.5in (34cm); tall hat with brim; long nose; raised circles around eyes and mouth; black painted pupil eyes; white painted teeth; face, mask, body, limbs totally painted in designs of black and white shapes on ochre background; holds fiber whisks in hands. Made by Herbert Sandala, a dancer. **Mother (Kalue):** 13in (33cm); burlap body; fiber dress painted black with ochre lines and white square shapes over a wire; neck, arms, and flat wide feet are painted with horizontal ochre, white and black stripes; face mask has raised circles around eyes and mouth; large, long nose; black pupil eyes; white feathers are sewn to top of heads; holds fiber whisks in hands. **Son (Chikuze):** 15in (38cm); painted mask head; fine lines and shapes on pointed hat with a pointed tassel; long curved nose with black red and ochre vertical lines; raised circles around eyes and mouth; black painted pupils; shaped and painted fiber teeth protrude from mouth; painted ochre, white, black lines encircle limbs; black painted torso decorated with white and ochre triangular shapes and swirls; holds fiber tassels; 1994.

The Makishi found in Angola, Zaire, Zambia and North Zimbabwe, do various dances for hunting lion, hyena, and other animals. Each dancer makes his own costume masks so no one knows who it is. The Makishi women do not dance. They clap and sing. Men dress and act as women. When they move their bodies, the stripes move also. *Sherry Morgan Collection.* **MARKS:** "Herbert Sandala" on bottom of feet.

#69. Sculpture Garden of the National Gallery in Harare: The native people of Zimbabwe are known for their stone sculpture. This picture was taken in the National Gallery in Harare. Small stone sculptures are available and for sale at the Gallery and are additions to international doll collections. *Photography by Harriet Beerbas, Dollco.*

69

ASIAN

See page 149 for more information about this doll.

AFGHANISTAN

Afghanistan, a country in the middle of Asia, borders Russia, Iran, India and Pakistan. It is home to over 16,450,000 people of different ethnic backgrounds. Islam is the chief religion. The dolls shown are from different parts of the country. Each region has different "national" costumes. Some dolls have tags explaining costumes.

Many women do not wear the chadri, although they wear a scarf over their head. After they are married, women wear their hair braided down their backs. Their dress is knee length or below with ankle-length harem pants and shoes with upturned toes. Often their clothes have beautiful embroidered decorations.

The men wear full, wrapped pantaloons with a loose tunic of white cotton. They often wear a red embroidered waistcoat. Their turbans require 6 to 9 yards of material which is wound carefully so that the forehead is bare to touch the ground when praying to Allah.

70

#70. ***LEFT to RIGHT:*** **Afghanistan Couple:** 7.5in (19cm); mask faces; vinyl bodies. **Lady:** wears a simple, bright, multi-colored print dress; long light cotton black veil; two red sequins earrings; bright red cotton pants; late 1960s. **Man:** wears a black robe with cap sleeves; green shirt under robe; long whiskers; white turban; late 1960s. The original owner was visiting an American teacher in a native school. She purchased both dolls in the native market. **MARKS:** None.

71

#71. A *chart of Afghanistan dolls* serves as a costume explanation of the pictured ones. The picture shows four dolls of the set of eight. ***LEFT to RIGHT:***
Pushtana: 10.5in (27cm); all cloth; hand embroidered face; glass earrings; navy blue dress: 1950s. **MARKS:** "This is the national dress of the women of Afghanistan. The bodice is embroidered with many colored stones, bangles or small mirrors depending on the area from which it comes. This costume has never been covered by the chadri."
Mullah: 6in (15cm) in sitting position; all cloth; white garb and turban of a religious man. **MARKS:** "The Mullah is a religious scholar who leads the Muslims in prayer. The Holy Koran is reverently held in two hands and never placed on the floor. Muslims say their prayers on a prayer rug. During moments of meditation a tasbih (prayer beads) which he is holding in his hands is used."
Jubiwal: 10.5in (27cm); all cloth. **MARKS:** "This is a man from the southern province of Afghanistan. He is doing the Atan, the national dance. His hair, deliberately left long for the dance, can be heard swishing through the air with his leaps and twirls as the tempo of the drum gains momentum." He also swirls two chiffon scarfs in the air at the same time. He wears a costume similar to the Pushtana but also wears a red velvet bolero trimmed in gold.
Pushtana: 10.5in (27cm); all cloth; earrings are multi-colored beads. **MARKS:** "This is the national dress of the women of Afghanistan. The bodice is embroidered in silver and gold and sometimes includes colored stone, bangles, or small mirrors, depending on the area from which it comes. This costume has never been covered by the chadri."
GiGi Williams Collection.

BANGLADESH

Bangladesh is encircled by India except for a small area of Burma (Myanmar) and an outlet on the Bay of Bengal in the south. It is a dry country with an annual monsoon flood season. The majority of Bangladeshi are Sunni Muslims but there are a few Shiite Muslims.

Speaking the Bengali language, Bangladeshi are closely related to the Indians and wear the same type of clothing. There would not be much difference in their dolls.

They do have a few tribal groups, especially in the Chittagong Hills of the southeast. Other groups are Buddhists, Christians, or animists. They, too, wear the same type of clothes as the people of India belonging to the same religion.

Speaking the Bengali language, Bangladeshi are closely related to the Indians and wear the same type of clothing. With little difference between their dolls, unless one is actually marked, it is difficult to determine whether it is from Bangladesh or India.

72

#72. Two Women Snake Charmers: 2in (5cm) high; 4in (10cm) high; tan with orange rim straw mat; women made of straw; black thread hair; woman on right has black dress with purple flowers; pink sleeves; woman on left has green dress with brighter green sleeves; red hairband; snake is black and white straw; 1900s. **MARKS:** None.

BURMA *(Myanmar)*

Like most of the Indo-Asian Countries, Burma's population is made up of many different ethnic groups. Religion, politics, life-styles, jobs, education and clothing all depend on the heritage of the person. Burma is surrounded by Bangladesh, India, China, Laos, and Thailand.

The ethnic groups include the Shans, Karens, Mons, Arakanese, Kachins, Chins, Kayahs, and Padaungs. All seven speak Burmese. The most popular religion is Buddhism.

Both male and female Burmans wear the *lonyi*, a wrap-around skirt worn folded across the front and gathered in. Men tie it in a knot. The women tuck in the ends. A blouse or shirt is worn with the *lonyi*. A type of shirt jacket called *eingyi* is worn outside. These are made of cotton or silk or a mixture of both.

Hat fashions include: flat straw hats worn by both men and women and colored handkerchiefs tied around men's heads. In Shan territory, turbans are worn by the men. The women wear folded white headscarfs or turbans.

The Kachin women wear black skirts edged with a red panel tied around the waist with a blue sash. They may wear a black long-sleeved jacket over white or black blouses. They also wear many strings of beads. Their hats are tall and black with large circular silver earrings.

Lashi women from Kachin wear similar costumes but in blue and white with blue turbans and necklaces of red beads.

The Black Lisu tribe women wear a tight-fitting cap made of red bead strings, white buttons, and tiny brass bells across their forehead.

The Padaung women from Kayah have the "giraffe" neck of circular rings that some tribes in Africa use to extend their necks. The word Padaung means "long neck". The girls have a special ceremony when they are five and have one ring installed. More are added until they have 21. Brass rings are also placed around their legs, extending from the ankles to above the knees. Their dress is a short, dark blue skirt edged with red, a loose white tunic trimmed with red, and a short blue jacket. A headscarf wound like a turban is their head wear.

73

#73. Burma Lady: 4in (10cm); vase-like black wood body; painted face; black hair; ornate red, silver, gold ribbon trim; yellow cord for headdress; rings around neck; 1984. **MARKS:** "Burma".

CHINA

One of the most exotic countries on earth is the lovely and diverse Republic of China. The people, the customs, and dolls are probably among the least known to the modern western world.

Today Chinese dolls from the 19th century are rarely found even in Chinese museums. This is because China was a very crowded land, and people could not have many possessions in their small homes. They enjoyed traveling puppet shows, and we know that their children played with "paper" dolls of many kinds over the years.

The earliest surviving dolls seem to come from the beginning of this century. The Chinese grandmothers talk of "playing house" with papier mâché-type composition dolls that they were not able to keep as adults. The Chinese do not comprehend the concept of doll collecting as we know it in the Western World and in Japan.

Some of the early dolls were made in the Christian missions to provide work for the indigent people. A wonderful example is the doll of the Mission of Hope of Shanghai, China. There were many other dolls made for export and the tourist trade during this century.

The early writers of doll books speculated about this lack of dolls. Some even thought it was a "taboo". Later writers spoke about the lack of dolls seen with children. When Polly went to China she, too, did not see children with dolls, but she quickly learned that the children love toys. Today dolls may be purchased in toy and department stores throughout China. However, by law, children are not allowed to carry toys with them on the streets because in the traffic and congestion they might get hurt. They do have dolls, toys, and stuffed animals at home to play with in the inner courtyards of the housing developments.

The Chinese section is divided into two parts. 1. The traditional Chinese dolls made mostly for export during this century. 2. The type of dolls available to Chinese children today.

#74. Chinese Boy: 8in (20cm); composition; dressed in red silk heavily embroidered coat and orange embroidered pants; red silk tiny shoes with gold braid; hat has beads and a Chinese coin; another coin dangling from his ear; 1920s–1930s. **MARKS:** None.

For the meaning of mythological symbols used in the costumes of dolls, see page 163.

74

#75.Chinese Marionettes: The man and woman represent a very wealthy Chinese couple; 6in (15cm); composition heads and hands; cloth bodies. The man's "flag-like" headdress is purple and white; the rest of his costume is multi-colored satin. The wife is also wearing a multi-colored satin dress; 1983. **MARKS:** None.

75

76

#76. Chinese Family: These are figures representing a Chinese family. They are made of clay. Each face is different, and the clothes are representative of the age of the member of the family; early 1900s. *Yoshika Baker Collection.* **MARKS:** None.

77

#77. Hand Carved Chinese Ricksha: made from redwood; carved seat, fenders, wheels with spokes that turn; separately carved folded top; umbrella; fan; pulled by wooden poles which go through the hands of the puller. Puller and seated man also entirely hand carved. The one-of-a-kind rickshaw was made in the 1980s in the Zhejiang Province near Shanghai, but was purchased in October 1991. It can be compared to the older example also made in China *(see page 59, bottom).* *Sherry Morgan Collection.* **MARKS:** None.

#78. Kneeling Warrior: 5.5in (14cm); terra cotta replica of the Qin Shi Huangdi tomb figures discovered in 1974; exquisitely executed, life-like representation of Chinese art 2,000 years ago. The replica figures have just begun to "surface" at doll, toy, and collectible shows and in art galleries. **MARKS:** None.

78

79

#79. ***LEFT to RIGHT:*** **Elderly Chinese Man:** 12.5in (32cm); painted features; long white beard; modeled hat with gilt decoration; silk Chinese costume over rolled paper body; papier mâché limbs; wooden base; 1920s. **MARKS:** "Made in China" on base. **Horse and Rider:** 10in (25cm); horseback rider from Chinese Opera; gofum over crushed wood base; red costume heavily embroidered with gold; carrying large spear; wooden painted legs to imitate boots; stiff papier mâché horse with red and black decorations; 1920s. **MARKS:** "Made in China". **Dancer from Traditional Chinese Opera:** 8.5in (22cm); stiff papier mâché base; multi-colored flowers on head-piece; red, green sleeves with black and gold striped cuffs; red and yellow kimono trimmed in wire decoration; with yellow fringe at bottom; 1920s. **MARKS:** None. *Shirley Karaba Collection.*

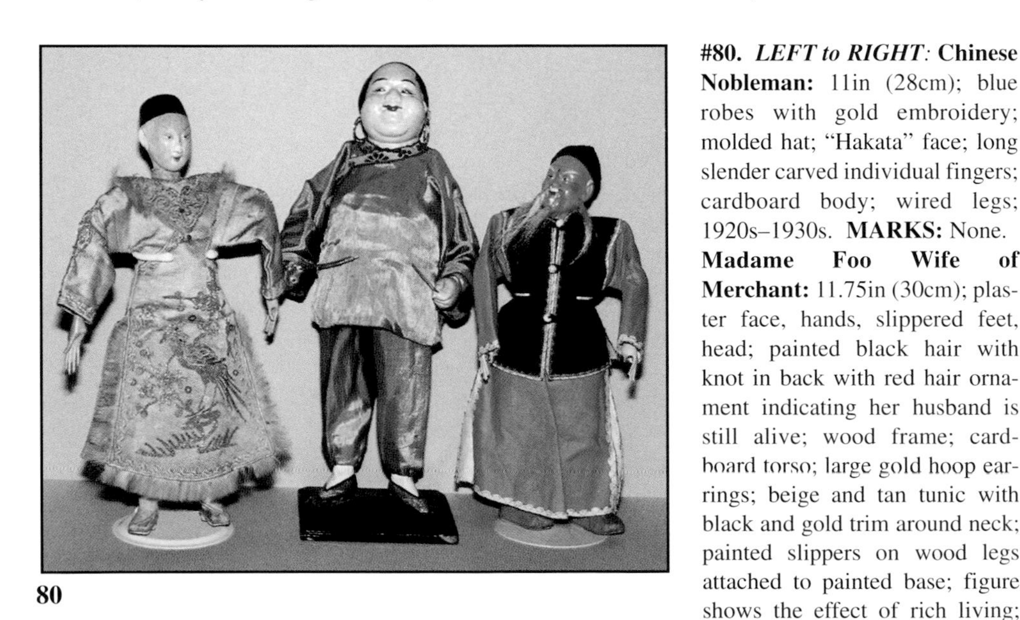

80

#80. ***LEFT to RIGHT*****:** **Chinese Nobleman:** 11in (28cm); blue robes with gold embroidery; molded hat; "Hakata" face; long slender carved individual fingers; cardboard body; wired legs; 1920s–1930s. **MARKS:** None. **Madame Foo Wife of Merchant:** 11.75in (30cm); plaster face, hands, slippered feet, head; painted black hair with knot in back with red hair ornament indicating her husband is still alive; wood frame; cardboard torso; large gold hoop earrings; beige and tan tunic with black and gold trim around neck; painted slippers on wood legs attached to painted base; figure shows the effect of rich living; 1920s–1930s. **MARKS:** None. **Old Man (Possibly Opera Character):** 10in (25cm); cotton body; black cap with beige pom pom on top; black sleeveless jacket with beige trim and buttons down the front; dark tan robe with white and green trim; leather shoes. **MARKS:** None. *Shirley Karaba Collection.*

81

#81. ***LEFT to RIGHT:*** **Opera Characters:** 9in (23cm); painted papier mâché head and hands; cloth-over-armature body; multi-colored costume; 1980s. Chinese Opera does not rely on scenery but the costumes, gestures, and words to tell the story. It takes years to learn the exact movements to express feelings as well as tell the story. **MARKS:** "Made in China" on the bottom of the box. **The Flying Horse of Kansu:** A replica of the original flying horse made in bronze; made soon after the original was brought to the U.S. for an exhibition at the National Gallery of Art in Washington, D.C. December 1974 to March 1975; now exhibited in a China museum. Dated 2nd Century A.D., the horse was found with a group of other bronzes from an Eastern Han Tomb in Wuwei, Kansu Province. **MARKS:** None.

#82. ***LEFT to RIGHT:*** **Monkey King Puppet:** 12in (31cm); papier mâché head; cloth body; tall headdress decorated with red stitching, blue top with silver trim; gaudy highly decorated robe with turquoise, red, yellow, green, white colors; 1980s. **Dragon:** 9in (23cm) long gold wire wound around cloth form; head decorated with pink wire and large pearl; each antenna has a pearl at the end; 1980s. The dragon is seen at the festivals cavorting in the streets, especially at the New Year's Festival.
MARKS: None.

82

83

#83. Six Chinese Character Dolls: 6in (15cm); Chinese composition head, hands, and feet; rolled up paper and wire bodies; excellent painted features; clothes all original. ***LEFT to RIGHT:*** **Lady with Pipe:** elaborate scarf covering white hair; red hair with gray streaks in it; red hair ornament with blue stick holds back of two-tiered bun; oriental eyes and painted furrows; maroon top; blue pants. **Another Lady with Pipe:** blonde hair; black head scarf with blue decorations and bands to hold scarf over buns; wire earrings; dark blue top with light colored pants. **Fisherman:** gray hair in a bun; black headpiece; holds silver fish with net. **Man in Blue Silk Kimono***:* Gray streaked hair; red ornament. **Shaved Head Man:** black eyebrows; unusual mouth; light green silk kimona with white collar; holding red sticks. **Shaved Head Man:** red kimono with white collar; head thrown back with mouth wide open as if singing (or screaming). *Marge Hunter Collection.* **MARKS:** "CHINA" stamped on some of their feet.

84

#84. ***LEFT to RIGHT:*** **Chinese Lady:** 9.5in (24cm); head, arms, and upper half of body are Chinese composition, sanded and painted a cream color; legs are paper rolled over wire armature. The top of her silk costume is blue with printed trim and hand embroidery; pants are pink silk with blue trim; shoes are painted red and black. An excellent condition 70 year old doll. **MARKS:** None on doll. **Chinese Lady:** 9.5in (24cm); doll has same body characteristics as one on left; painted black hair and molded bun; painted blue scarf with black trim; dark blue tunic with intricate red and cream embroidery trim down front of the dress and around the large sleeves; beige silk skirt; 1920s. **MARKS:** "Made in China" on bottom of stand.

#85. China and Cloth Character Dolls: 15in (38cm); heads, lower arms and legs of china; upper arms, upper legs, and torso of cloth; heads do not swivel; 1920s -1930s. ***LEFT to RIGHT:*** **Man:** open mouth; pierced nostrils; glasses; yellow hat with black band; blue satin tunic; red satin vest with frog closings; left hand cupped with hole to hold an item. **Captain:** pierced nostrils; blue satin tunic; white shirt; red tie; black hat. **Child:** open mouth, pierced nostrils; red dress with decorations around arms; blue top with red diamond pattern; pigtails; figure indicates wealth. **Lady:** pierced nostrils and ears with earrings; blue satin dress with white trim. China-made doll set was purchased in Nuremberg, Germany in 1989 in an Oriental shop run by a German man. *Bill Zito Collection.* **MARKS:** Unknown.

85

#86. Chinese Noble Man and Woman Pulled In Ricksha. Ricksha: 11in (28cm) and 14in (36cm); metal construction; heavy tarpaulin-type material for pull-out tops; metal lanterns on each side; late 1800s-early 1900s. **MARKS:** None. **Noble Woman:** 8in (20cm); baked clay; cloth upper body; arms and legs attached to metal armature; ornate headpiece with baked clay decorations; black silk print top; pink silk skirt; red painted shoes; late 1800s-early 1900s. **Noble Man:** 12in (31cm) composition head, and long, slim fingers; inserted eyes; painted mustache; ornate red, embroidered court dress; blue cloth appliqued with gold thread, cream satin cuffs on sleeves and around bottom of robe; lined with red and white cotton print; Chinese cloth shoes carefully painted and sewn; paper headdress decorated with red and gold paper ornaments; 1920s. **Ricksha pullers:** composition heads with molded Coolie hats; composition hands and feet; cloth body; arms and legs attached to armature in body; wires in hands to hold rickshas. **MARKS:** None.

86

87

#87. Antique Chinese Opera Dolls: 31in (79cm); papier mâché; all silk costumes; unusually long fingernails which are indications that these characters represent nobility; 1800s. All three dolls positioned for their opera parts. **LEFT to RIGHT: Servant:** white tunic with blue and pink trim on dress and red, blue, pink, green trim on large sleeves; pink brocade pants; wooden shoes; simple blue headdress. **Leading Character***:* ornate dress with papier mâché lion dog at her waist and monkeys below; white dress with multi-colored heavy embroidery; high ornate headdress with fruit and feathers; wooden shoes. **Nobleman:** blue and white shirt over white pants; red trim; flat hair decoration in same colors; wooden shoes. **MARKS:** Chinese characters on bottom of base.
Shirley Lindner Collection.

88

#88. Chinese Bride: excellent composition head, hands, feet; cloth body; black human hair rolled into braided buns over ears and bangs on forehead; thin brass headpiece decorated with pom poms and colored streamers over face; dark red and blue brocade; green trim jacket; frog closings; bright red brocade pleated skirt; blue satin long pants; painted red shoes with blue decoration; smiling, beautiful bride. 1930s. *Sandy Strater Collection.* **MARKS:** None.

89

#89. Antique Chinese Opera Dolls: Same characteristics as the dolls on *page 60, top*. ***LEFT to RIGHT:*** **Young Man:** Multicolored under garment; pink, red, blue, gold pants; gold crown on head; wooden shoes; heavily embroidered coat; probably a *Prince*. **Young Woman:** embroidered scalloped collar; multi-colored fringe hangs from her heavily embroidered coat; wooden shoes; probably a *Princess*. **Monkey King:** pink coat with ornate blue trim; matching short pants; high "*Monkey King*" boots. His face makeup is similar to other *Monkey Kings* in this book. Over 200 or more chinese operas with the Monkey King as the lead character. *Shirley Lindner Collection.* **MARKS:** Chinese figures on the base.

#90. Musical Girl: carved from ox horn; cloisonné girl holding a gold-toned horn; black hair in elaborate swirls, top knot and bangs; carved eyes; black painted pupils; face is slightly blushed; pink rosebud mouth; carved earrings; sleeve and sash hanging from waist; body and clothing are in cloisonné; front of coat and edge of left sleeve have purple cloisonné flowers on blue background; upper part of coat and rest of sleeves have large blue and green flowers on yellow enamel; red enamel sash; front lower part of coat has two tones of blue enamel and gold lines forming diamond shapes; skirt is light green enameled flowers with chains holding a gold pendant of red enamel flowers; purchased in Chanquig, China. The figurine's story is that she is one of a family of four girls, each of whom is a musician. *Sherry Morgan Collection.*
MARKS: None.

90

91

#91. ***LEFT to RIGHT:*** **Monkey King:** 13in (33cm) with hat; papier mâché head and legs to knee; long fingers; wire armature body with cardboard over chest portion of body; gold molded papier mâché crown with ornate flowers and decorations; purple silk coat with elaborate gold trim, green panels and sleeves with embroidery; red silk skirt over beige printed silk pants; purple velvet shoes. **MARKS:** Chinese writing molded into head. **Old Woman:** 10.5in (27cm) with hat; baked clay molded face with wrinkles; wire armature body with cardboard around chest area; long fingers; gold earrings; mandarin-type blue silk hat over gray and white striped material to indicate gray hair; beige heavily embroidered silk tunic slitted at both sides; blue embroidered silk pants; green embroidered shoes. **MARKS:** Chinese writing molded into head. **Younger Woman:** 11in (28cm); sculptured, painted clay head; slitted painted black eyes; high arched eyebrows; burlap-type body; light composition-type hands with long fingers; ornate headpiece with beads, gold cloth decoration; gold earrings; white tunic with red, green, gold thread on heavy satin; blue satin pants with gold embroidery; wooden legs; orange and black painted shoes. *Sandra Strater Collection.* **MARKS:** Chinese writing molded into head. **Military Man:** sculptured, painted clay head with inset black eyes; wire armature body with wood around chest area; heavy cloth Chinese armor-type uniform embroidered in beautiful designs; cotton print pants; heavy wooden shoes with upturned toes. **MARKS:** Chinese writing molded into head.

#92. ***LEFT to RIGHT:*** **Monkey King:** 18in (46cm); molded, heavy composition head; real white hair and beard; dressed in yellow, pink, white cloth with glitter; 1920s-1930s. **Emperor:** 21in (53cm); heavy composition head; real, black hair and mustache; clothes not as glittery, made with colorful brocade fabrics. The puppets are very heavy and must have been difficult to use during the actual play or opera; 1930s. **Five Cornean Lions:** 4in (10cm) x 4in (10cm); molded, painted lay body; yarn simulated fur; claws made of stiff bristles; head on spring which moves paper tongue when jiggled; the usual defenders of Buddhist altars and temples; also called Dog of Foo or Dog of Buddha. **MARKS:** None on any of the dogs or puppets.

92

93

#93. Pa-Hsien, The Eight Immortals: Chinese mythology characters who have become immortal through the practice of the Taoist doctrine. The shown immortals are spirits who are deified and dwell in the mountains and hills away from human beings. They are presumed to have the power of being visible or invisible at will, of raising the dead, or changing anything they touch to gold. Folklore did not include their names until the Yuan dynasty about the 13th or 14th century. Their importance spread through Chinese theatre. Differences in name spellings and sculptor's interpretations are apparent.

(Left to Right): **Quan Yin** the Goddess of Love and Mercy (not part of the the Eight Immortals): 7in (18cm); chinese carved teakwood; Patron Saint of Chinese housewife.

Immortals: approximately 8in (20cm); Chinese carved teakwood.

1. **Chung Li Chuan** represents wisdom.
2. **Tu Tung Ping** represents health.
3. **Chang Kuo-Lao** represents courage.
4. **Htjaew-uh Cux Oast** represents wealth.
5. **Plebianism**
6. **Han Hsiang Tze** represents youth.
7. **Lan-tsai-Ho** represents contentment.
8. **Ho-hsien-kiu** represents femininity.

Immortals spelled differently (not in same order) in the April 1943 issue of Kimport's *Doll Talk:*

1. Han Chung Li.
2. Lilieh Kuai.
3. Lung Tung Pin.
4. Lan Tsai-Ho.
5. Tsai Juo Chiw.
6. Chang Kuo Lao.
7. Han Hsian-TZE.
8. Ho Hsien-Ku.

MARKS: None.

Thelma Purvis Collection.

DOLLS OF THE DOOR OF HOPE MISSION

Started in Shanghai 1900 by a group of women missionaries, the mission sheltered orphans, destitute widows and any young women needing help. The missionaries educated both the children and women in the morning, and in the afternoon taught them to sew as an occupation. This led to doll production, mostly for export to the United States. These dolls were well carved from pearwood which matched the Chinese fleshtone.

When the women and girls became proficient enough to make clothes for the dolls, they were paid three to five cents an hour. The early dolls were sold for $.75-5.00 which was expensive for the time. It took one sewer about one month to clothe the doll.

The doll clothes were fashioned meticulously with tiny stitches modeling the fashions of the Chinese clothes. Since the dolls were made for almost half a century, the fashions changed with the times. For instance, after 1914 the hair queue of the men and the bound feet of the women were no longer part of the Chinese culture or the dolls. Although, for the most part, the types of dolls remained the same, *Door of Hope* collectors enjoy the changes in Chinese fashions.

World War II interfered with the shipment of these dolls to the U.S. and neither Kimport or Elsie Krug, both doll importers, received any new dolls after 1939. It is estimated that from 1902-1939 there were about 50,000 made.

All Door of Hope dolls have carved peachwood heads, lower arms and hands; inset painted eyes; cloth bodies; and a similar type of underware.

For further information the authors highly recommend a little yellow booklet called "Doll Talk" from Kimport. They are not only helpful with *Door of Hope* dolls, but they are full of information which can help you identify many other dolls. Kimport is no longer in business.

DOOR OF HOPE DOLLS

1. **Amah**
2. **Amah and Baby**
3. **Baby**
4. **Bride**
5. **Bridegroom**
6. **Buddhist Priest**
7. **Girl in Silk**
8. **Farmer**
9. **Kindergarten Child**
10. **Manchu Woman**
11. **Modern Bride in Pink**
12. **Mourner** (Man)
13. **Old Lady and Gentleman**
14. **Policeman**
15. **School Boy in Cotton**
16. **School Girl in Cotton**
17. **Small Boy in Silk**
18. **Small Girl in Silk**
19. **Tableboy**
20. **Widow**
21. **Young Lady**
22. **Young Lady in Long Garment**

For examples of Door of Hope dolls see illustrations 95 and 96, page 65.

#94. ***LEFT to RIGHT:*** **Mother and Child Pebbles Doll:** 5in (13cm); made from varnished pebbles; heads of mother and child are painted pebbles; black hair with extra pebble for bun on woman; painted face; larger pebble for body painted blue, yellow and red for clothes; arms suggested by shape of stone to be holding a baby; long, thin, black pebble used to suggest bottom of dress; doll glued to white tile. **MARKS:** None originally. **Man Holding Peach**: 5in (13cm) with base; pebble head with painted features and hat; wool beard glued on face; green painted coat with flowers; long pink sleeves; two black painted pebbles for feet glued to black pebble base. **MARKS:** None.
Sherry Morgan Collection.

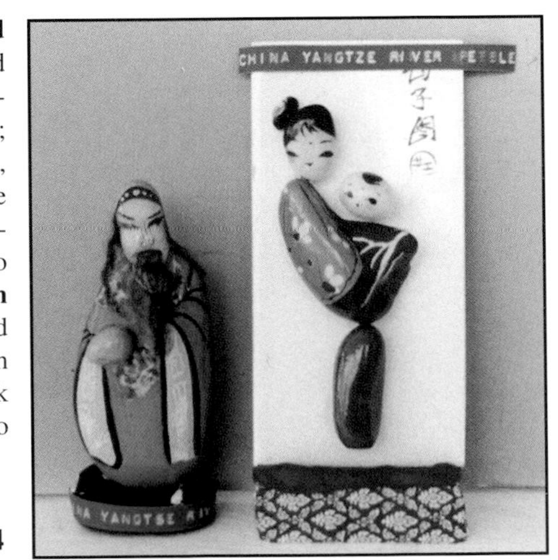

94

#95. ***LEFT to RIGHT:*** **Widow:** 11in (28cm); cloth body; painted black hair with unusual unpainted "u-shaped" line in center of forehead; single hair bun with no decoration because she is a widow; unbleached muslin trousers under side-gored, fringed skirt; frog fastened blouse; sack-cloth fingertip jacket with frog closings and tied rope belt; sack-cloth lined shoulder-length head covering with piece of red cloth sewn to crown in back; sack cloth shoes over pointed feet indicating bound feet; 1920s or before. **Amah and Baby:** 11in (28cm) white smock with blue frog closings; black painted hair; blue brocade trousers; baby tied to back with red square piece of material; red rope belt. **Baby:** 5in (13cm); baby is dressed in green, white, yellow, orange print; red satin slippers with turquoise embroidery; embroidered hat with white fringe; multi-colored ball on top. *Beverly Findlay Collection.* **Boy:** 7.5in (19cm); green brocade leggings (trousers); sleeveless white cotton inner shirt with side-closing frogs; long side closing pink silk brocade robe with green trim and frogs; red embroidered Chinese-type slippers with upturned toes; round, gored brimless hat with red trim on top; blue heavily embroidered inner hat; round black painted hair with hair queue (pigtail down to his waist in back); long bangs down to eyes in front; 1914. **Young Gentleman:** 11in (28cm); dark blue overjacket with frog closing; light blue side fastening silk brocade robe; dark trousers and thigh-length robe fastened to top with strings; crotch is open; black brimless hat with red pom pom on top; black silk shoes with blue soles and turned up toe; part of it is machine stitched; after 1920. **Young Lady:** 10.75in (27cm); raw blue silk brocade overjacket with frog side closings; white blouse; light blue brocaded pants with white and blue piping around bottom; double braided buns over ears; tiny bound feet with hand embroidered shoes; all hand sewn; Pre-1920s. *Sandra Strater Collection.* **MARKS:** No identification marks on any of the dolls.

95

*Frogs are a cloth ball and loop-type fastener for clothing.

#96. Door of Hope Manchu Nobleman-Groom: 12in (31cm); deep purple silk outer robe fully lined in blue cotton; back and both sides have traditional Chinese slits in the hem of the robe; long sleeves; four black frog closings; on front and back of robe are hand embroidered pink and aqua flowers, show family social status; silk brocade inner coat with two side slits; fully lined with mauve cotton and black frog closures; small Chinese collar with black edging; white cotton undershirt and underpants held up by a cord; legs covered with white silk; purple silk boots; about 1912. *Sherry Morgan Collection.* **MARKS:** Chinese figures on Undershirt; #5 marked in pencil on bottom of lining of coat; #17 on blue lining of coat; #34 on each leg.

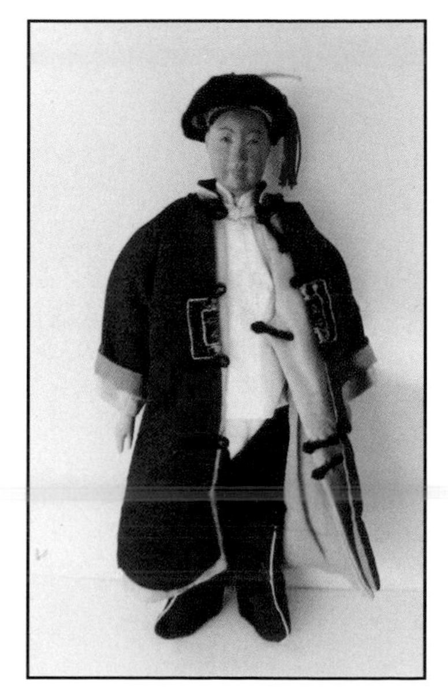

96

97

#97. Mongolian Doll in Red: 18in (46cm); vinyl doll; molded hair and facial features; heavy flannel side-fastened coat trimmed with fur; matching hat; blue ribbon around her waist; heavy, red vinyl boots. **MARKS:** None.

#98. Modern Lao-tze, A Squeeze Toy: 9in (23cm); all vinyl; 1983. Lao-tze was the founder of Taoism. A contemporary of Confucius, Lao-tze is associated with legends of immortality and the power to conquer demons. This doll is a puckish mythological character who attacks the horrible dragon that is devastating the lands of the poor people. Made as a child's toy to be given as a reminder of the caring attitude. **MARKS:** None.

98

99

#99. Young Traveler: vinyl doll; yellow molded cap; white shirt; dark blue pants; metal suitcase with windup mechanism which makes the doll walk at a fast gait when it is wound. **MARKS:** None on doll; box says "Young Traveler".

#100. Modern Girl and Boy: 11in (28cm); silk mask faces, cloth bodies, jointed at shoulders and hips; 1980s. ***LEFT to RIGHT:*** **Girl:** black thread hair with bangs and pigtails; red pajama-type suit with black designs and gold embroidery; matching red shoes. **Boy:** blue velvet hat; gold and black brocade top; dark blue brocade skirt; turquoise pants; black brocade shoes. *Sandra Strater Collection.* **MARKS:** None.

100

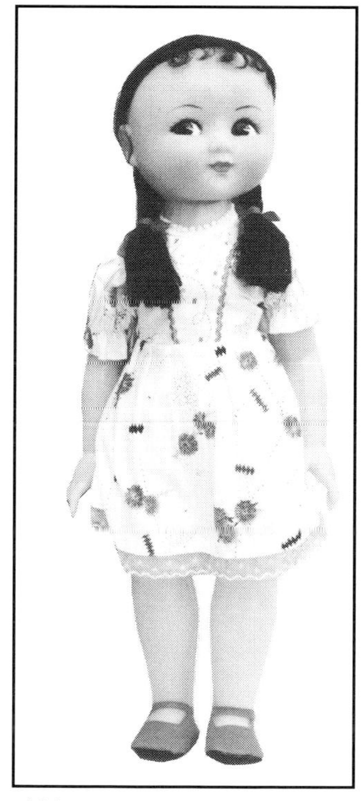

101

#101. Doll from Xian: 17in (43cm); flexible vinyl head; rooted black hair; stiff waxy vinyl body; painted eyes; white dress with red and pink flowers; gold rickrack trim; embroidered ribbon around hem of red-leather-like shoes with pearl fastener; 1983. **MARKS:** None.

102

#102. ***LEFT to RIGHT:*** **Bride:** 10in (25cm); hard cone body; soft vinyl face; blonde synthetic hair; painted face; red silk bouffant wedding dress trimmed with white lace; white organdy collar; bridal bouquet of white, blue, yellow flowers; sparkling trim glued onto dress; matching headdress; 1983. **Groom:** 12in (31cm); hard vinyl body; same face and hair as Bride; modern black twill suit; velvet collar; red velvet tie; red and pink boutonniere; red velvet hat with gold trim on brim and on top; couple purchased at the largest Department Store in Shanghai, China. **MARKS:** None on doll.

103

#103. Dolls from Various Provinces: toy set of six provincial heads; used to teach Chinese geography to children; small size allows for easy storage; sold in red unmarked box in Chinese toy stores. **MARKS:** "Made in the People's Republic of China" on the side of the box.

104

#104. Three Chinese Opera Masks: 5in (13cm); baked clay faces with real hair beards; sold in a flat box for use as wall decorations in the small living quarters of the people of Kweilin (Guilin) in the southern part of China bordering North Korea. The middle doll is the *Monkey King*. The doll on the right is the *God of the Earth and Temple Guardian.* **MARKS:** None.

105

#105. Panda: 7in (18cm); made from fluffy, furry Chinese material; vinyl eyes; carrying a white and orange ball with a red spot in the center; purchased at Peking Zoo. The Chinese love to take their children to the zoo to see the pandas. **MARKS:** None.

#106. ***LEFT to RIGHT:*** **Chinese Boy in Sitting Position with Cymbals:** 6in (15cm); clay head with human hair pigtails sticking up from head; cloth body; yellow robe; orange scarf; red belt and red trim in center of cymbals; velvet shoes. **MARKS:** "Handmade in Taiwan//Republic of China" seal on back of foot. **Chinese Walking Boy:** 10.5in (27cm); composition painted head and lower arms; wooden body; wood legs which move as if walking; pink Chinese brocade robe with side ties; matching pants; black silk robe with frog closings; black hat with pink brocade trim; 1930s. **MARKS:** None.

106

107

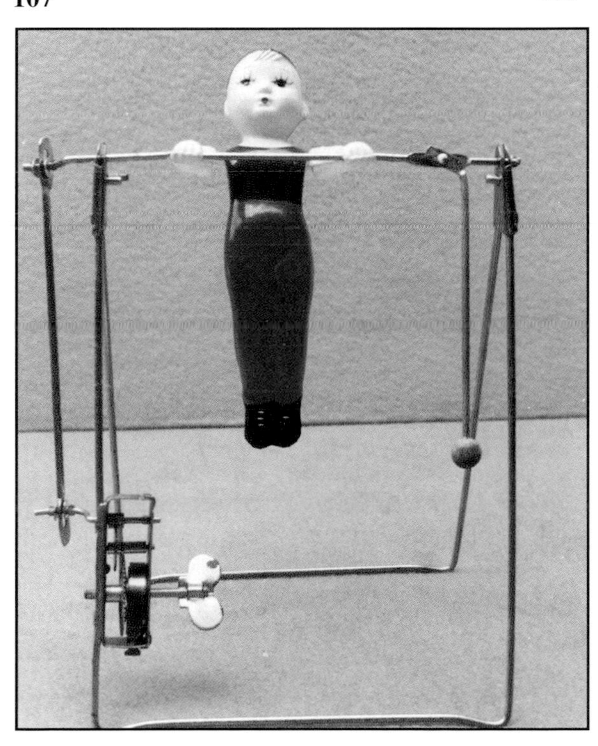

#107. Mechanical Gymnast: 5in (13cm) x 12.5in (31cm); hard vinyl doll; painted red and black single bar exercise suit; 1983. The children of China love wind-up mechanical toys. They particularly love a gymnast because gymnastics and acrobatics have both been theatre and street exhibitions for centuries in China. This toy has instructions in both Chinese and English in the box. **MARKS:** "Single Bar Exercise" on box.

108

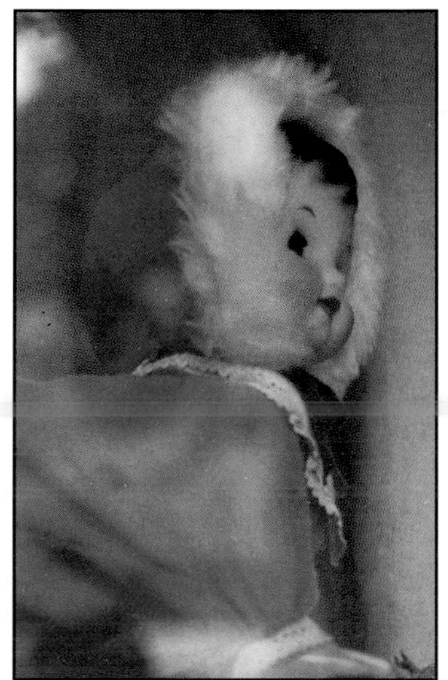

#108. Chinese Baby: 16in (41cm); all vinyl; pink dress and matching bonnet with white fur; wiggled and cried when activated by a whistle. She cost about $49 in Chinese money in 1983. Since the salary of the average worker was about $60 a month, some indulgent parent or grandparent must have saved long and hard to purchase her. This picture was taken in one of the Chinese toy stores that seemed to be in almost every block. **MARKS:** None.

109

#109. ***LEFT to RIGHT:*** **Chinese Provincial Costume:** 10in (25cm); waxy-type hard plastic head; vinyl body; smiling face nicely painted; thread hair combed into a double bun on head with three flowers as hair ornament; lavender Chinese tunic with red and black trim; white underblouse; multi-colored trim embroidered on arms, apron, deep pink pleated skirt; apron is made of netting with bird design woven into netting; pink satin slippers; 1982. **MARKS:** "Chinese National Costume" on box. **Chinese Doll in Traditional Costume:** 10in (25cm); waxy-type hard plastic; hard vinyl body; smiling face nicely painted; thread hair coiled into four buns in back of head surrounded by multi-colored flowers; pink and silver Chinese skirt; short green brocade jacket with black embroidery; red embroidered bag with yellow fringe carried by red strap over her shoulder; maroon plastic sandals; 1983. **MARKS:** "Made in the Peoples Republic of China" on box.

HONG KONG

At present, Hong Kong is a colony of Great Britain under a lease agreement. That lease will run out in 1997, and there is much speculation about what will happen when the colony becomes part of China again.

Although people from all over the world make their home in Hong Kong, the main culture has a Chinese base with Chinese, the language most often spoken by the people. English is understood.

Hong Kong Colony includes the island of Hong Kong, the city of Kowloon on the mainland across a narrow strait from the island, and the New Territories which touch the borders of China.

Hong Kong is one of the largest exporters of toys in the world. Along with United States-style dolls, they also make Chinese dolls and other Chinese art products such as the huge lion heads and dragons used in the parades during the holidays. They also export these to China and other countries that have Chinese residents. Many other countries around the world also have child dolls manufactured in Hong Kong.

#110. Beijing Opera Dolls: 10.5in (27cm); paper composition; silk and paper clothing. ***LEFT:*** white face with white blushed cheeks; simulated diamond on forehead; headdress has curly wire entwined with pearls, green and white pom poms, feathers and white tassels; four white triangular flaps decorated with pink foil birds are attached to back of doll; pink shoulder pads decorated with white fringe, silver foil and turquoise braid; yellow cloth collar; long white sleeves; at neck is red cloth peony with green, white, yellow cloth leaves from which hang orange strips; blue tassels; attached to a loop hangs a silver wire basket with cloth petals of blue, yellow and copper; the skirt has five panels which hang from waist; black ribbon and green folded panels decorate her costume in back; green shoes; holds long silver paper spear. ***RIGHT:*** orange painted face; almost the same costume in different colors; face is more accented; headdress has same materials but no feathers; green cloth over paper panel in back in slightly different design; doll holds gold foil mask and silver paper sword; green cloth over legs decorated with blue, gold, white strip of braid; 1993. Purchased in Hong Kong.
MARKS: Made in the People's Republic of China". *Sherry Morgan Collection.*

110

111

#111. Family Dolls: 5in (13cm); cloth bodies; painted features over painted wood; wooden hands; feet have Chinese shoes; blue, white, turquoise, pink brocade kimonos; dolls still tied in box; 1930s. *Nan Marie Grahanm and Lynn Bartol for Mary Jane's Dolls.*
MARKS: "With Chinese Figures Around the Cross// Service in Christ's Name//The Chinese Family//The Grandparents//The Child//The Prayer Circle//G.P.O. Box 893//Hong Kong B.C.C."

112

#112. Mao-type Clothes Worn by Chinese After the Communist Revolution: ***LEFT to RIGHT:*** **Woman:** 14in (36cm); all cloth; dark blue top and pants; frog closures; straw hat with black cotton hanging down; missing sandals; 1960s - 1970s. **Man:**14in (36cm); all cloth; wears blue suit with frog closings up the front of jacket; woven straw sandals; missing large straw hat; 1960s - 1970s. **MARKS:** "ADA LUM//Made in Hong Kong" on both dolls.

#113. Chieh-Chieh: 12in (31cm); cloth body on wooden stand; embroidered face; wearing bright red brocade and long gold dress trimmed with green satin and gold ribbon; slits up the side; crown-like red headpiece decorated with sequins, red pom poms, and yellow tassels; silk Chinese shoes; comes in white hand-woven basket; made by Lutheran World Service Crafts, Kowloon; 1970s. The doll has been difficult to find in the U.S. The scroll on the right in the basket explains the different costumes. **MARKS:** None on doll; in the box was a cloth tag with gold lettering, "Made by the Crafts Department of the Lutheran World Federation//Department of World Service//Hong Kong Office". The scroll was also included.

113

114

#114. All of the dolls are entirely made of cloth with embroidered faces, individual fingers; hand-made shoes of black cloth with white soles. ***LEFT to RIGHT:*** **Country Woman:** 10in (25cm); black cloth jacket with front frog closings; blue skirt with side frog closings. **Woman Carrying Boy:** 8in (20cm); green and white print cotton jacket with side frog closings; black pants; pink and white print around waist for carrying boy. **Boy:** 6in (15cm); shirt and pants made from yellow, red, black print; shirt has side frog closings. **Country Man:** 10in (25cm); black pants; dark blue jacket with side frog closings. **MARKS ON EACH DOLL:** "Tripod Marke//Made in Hong Kong//Chinese Doll" circular tag; on back of each tag is the name of the doll.

115

#115. ***LEFT to RIGHT:*** **Chinese Girl:** 10in (25cm); composition head, hands, feet; cloth and paper body; painted hair with human hair pigtails on each side of head; gold and pink embroidered figure on front of royal blue coat with pink trim; gold embroidery on pants; gold flower embroidered on back of coat; frog closings; removable red, trimmed shoes; 1930s.
MARKS: None. **Chinese Woman:** 9in (23cm) composition character face, legs; heavily stuffed cotton body; blue cotton brocade top with frog closings; black silk brocade long skirt; removable blue velvet shoes; molded papier mâché hat with glued gold ornaments; 1930s. **MARKS:** "China" on bottom of shoe. **Bow Bow:** 11in (28cm); composition head, hands, feet; cloth body; painted face; slits in composition for eyes; painted hands with pink fingernails; painted red shoes and white stockings; dressed in red and gold silk brocade coat; frog closings; green and gold brocade pants; red silk hat trimmed with green braid; metal decorations with Chinese symbols embossed on them; white pom poms on top of hat; on his left shoulder is a Hong Kong coin attached by a red string to his hat; brochure explains name and significance; 1930s. **MARKS:** "A MICHAEL LEE//CHINESE CHARACTER DOLL//MICALE//bow bow//MADE IN HONG KONG"

INDIA

India is so large that it is often called a subcontinent of Asia. Over 800 million people live here – that is about one out of every seven people in the world.

It is a land of many religions, races, languages, and castes. The Indians can determine their fellow men and women by appearance. Each group has its own style clothing, jewelry, facial makeup, hair style, and language. There are 15 different languages, often with different alphabets. The official language is Hindi and all school children take it. English is used in universities, government, science, and business.

There is a major division in the provinces between northern lighter skin Indians, and southern darker skin Indians. Each region or province's culture has different music, costumes, art, and predominate religion. Major religions include Buddhists, Christians, Hindu (majority), Jewish, Muslim (about 10%), Parsis, and Sikhs (the majority live in the state of Punjab). There are other religions, also.

Indians have great respect for education, art, beautiful buildings and monuments. However, because of poverty and crowded conditions, they have been migrating to many other countries all over the world.

PROVINCES OF INDIA

Three Broad Divisions

1. Deccan Plateau
2. The Himalayas "Land of Snow"
3. Indo-Gangetic Plain

PROVINCES

1. Jammu & Kashmir *, far north
2. Himachal Pradesh, north.
3. Sikkim, north.
4. Arunchal Pradesh, north.
5. Punjab, northwest.
6. Haryana, northwest.
7. Rajasthan (Brataphur), central west.
8. Utter Pradesh, north central.
9. Nagaland, northeast
10. Bihar, east central
11. West Bengal, north central.
12. Madhya Pradesh, central.
13. Gujarat, west central.
14. Orissa, east central.
15. Maharashtra, central.
16. Meghalaya, east central.
17. Mizoram, east central.
18. Manipur, northwest central.
19. Tripura, east central.
20. Andra Pradesh, southeast.
21. Karnataka, southwest.
22. Goa, southwest.
23. Tamil Nadu, far south.
24. Kerala, southwest.
25. Assam, far northwest.

*Kashmir disputed between India and Pakistan.

#116. ***LEFT to RIGHT:*** **Parci:** 12in (31cm); all cloth; mohair wig; painted face; large eyelashes; white spots on both sides of each eye; dressed in light cotton orange sari with gold trim; long veil in back. This lady belongs to the Parsi religion, one of the minor Indian religions. The Parsi fled from Persia to India. Today most of the Parsis live in and around the city of Bombay. **MARKS:** "Hand-Made India//Parsi; 1945."
Doll in Full Purdah: 10in (25cm); all cloth rose purdah clothes with white embroidery; unusually full covering. Carefully handcrafted doll. **MARKS:** None.

116

#117. ***LEFT to RIGHT:*** **Christa Mandir Doll:** 9in (23cm) cloth over armature; painted face with red dot on forehead; red short tunic with green plaid patches; blue skirt with red trim at bottom of skirt; long red chiffon scarf with white dots; 1960s. This doll is a Bhangra Dancer. **MARKS:** Bhat Embroidery//Christa Mandir//Dancing Doll." **Christa Mandir Doll:** 8.5in (22cm); stuffed cloth over armature; red dot of Hindu woman on forehead; blue bead necklace and nose ring; dark brown mohair hair with long pigtails; orange brocade tunic with red glass buttons; rust skirt with gold and yellow sequins and gold trim around bottom of skirt; 1960s. **MARKS:** "Christa Seva Mandir Doll – production circle, Siddeshwar Peth, Sholapur, India. Bhangra Dancer: This dance is specially performed in Punjasb state. During the festivals the men and women wear colorful clothes and dance together."

117

118

#118. LEFT to RIGHT: India Fish Lady: 12.5in (32cm); papier mâché head; cloth body; well-painted facial features with red dot on forehead; painted toenails and fingernails; real black hair; black cotton blouse; orange sari; silver earrings, bracelet, chain necklace, ankle rings; gold earrings; carrying a basket of fish. **MARKS:** "PRIYADARSHINI" stamped on bottom of base. **Punjabi, North India Bride:** 9.5in (24cm); molded ceramic shoulderplate and head; detailed facial painting; red dot on forehead; gold nose and forehead ornaments, bracelets, ring; several beaded necklaces; all fingers separate; red nails and red dots on the back of hands; red, white, green bodice; deep pink and black print skirt; yellow gauze shawl with green polkadots and gold trim; matching Indian pants; painted red shoes; circa 1975. **MARKS:** None on doll. **Hindu Woman:** 12in (31cm); all cloth; painted facial features; red dot of Hindu on forehead; pink and gray blouse; lavender sari with pink braid trim; bead bracelets and earrings; leather hand-sewn shoes; 1960s-1970s. **MARKS:** "Hand-made. India//6-0//Maharashtrian//RS. AS." oval arm tag. *Beverly Findlay Collection.*

119

#119. India Rajah Boy: 9in (23cm); all celluloid; bent limb baby; nicely painted face with black outlines around eyes; black dot in middle of forehead; gold brocade tunic and turban; stand-up decoration of shredded cloth with pearl ornament on hat; necklace of same material with emerald-colored stone at neckline; jeweled scmitar; gold belt; 1930s. *Sandy Strater Collection.* **MARKS:** "Holy Angels Convent//P.B. 107//Kumbakonam//(South India//No17 - Rajah//15-0-0" on tag as seen in picture.

120

#120. LEFT to RIGHT: Punjabi Bride: 9in (23cm); fired clay bodies; red chiffon bridal dress trimmed with gold; tunic with pants; shawl matches costume; gold ornaments in center of hair over forehead; gold ring on finger; face painted with three red dots surrounded by tiny white dots; silver ornaments hang from wrists; wearing sandals; 1970s. **MARKS:** "Punjabi Bride//Made in India." **Rajasthani Farmer:** 9in (23cm); fired clay body; Sikh religion; red print turban; turquoise short coat; white pants and shawl; ornament around neck; 1970s. **MARKS:** "Rajasthani Farmer//Made in India." **Bihari Village Woman:** 9in (23cm); fired clay body; carries a water jar; print sari and trouser outfit; barefoot; blue and gold bracelet, ring, necklace, and big pendant with stone in middle, earrings, and ornament in back of hair; 1970s. **MARKS:** Biheri Village Woman//Made in India. **Bride from Marwar (Jodhpur):** 5in (13cm); in sitting position; red dot on forehead; bright blue sari trimmed with gold fringe and other gold trimming; jewel on left side of nose; earrings, bracelets, rings; 1970s. **MARKS:** "Bride from Marwar (Jodhpur)" *Louise Schnell Collection.*

#121. Kerala Man: 20in (51cm); thick molded, painted papier mâché; constructed in three parts: head, upper and lower body. All three parts rest on a wire support which permits swaying and bobbing at the slightest breeze and makes the doll seem to dance. The doll holds rope which also moves as the doll sways. Kerala a coastal state on the Malabar strip in southern India, is known for its beautiful clothes and dance-drama performances. **MARKS:** None.

121

122

#122. I. Dolls from India Educational School kit. Although not pictured, the kit also contained miniature musical instruments, cooking utensils, and pamphlets about Indian provinces. The dolls, about 9in (23cm) tall, are all made of clay and were used in the 1950s. ***LEFT to RIGHT:*** **Rajasthan Lady from Northwest India:** red print skirt; lighter red sari; carrying jar on head and urn in arms; red dot on forehead; jeweled earrings, necklace bracelets and ankle ring; red short sari extending from top of head over hip. **Kashmir Muslim Lady:** pink print dress with matching pants tight at ankle; carrying a basket of food; head decorated with flowers; silver necklace, earrings, bracelets; carrying a basket of food. Kashmir borders on Tibet and China in the north. **Braham Lady from Madras:** flowers around hair which is pulled into a bun in back; jewelry includes earrings, necklace and bracelets; costume includes a short rust sari with gold threads and matching pants; long white veil on head. Madras, in South India borders the Bay of Bengal. **Hindu Woman Carrying Wood:** red dot on forehead; long yellow print tunic over pants. *Carlton Brown Collection.* MARKS: None on the dolls.

123

#123. II. Dolls from India Educational Kit: ***LEFT to RIGHT:*** **Hindu Woman with Red Dot on Forehead:** wearing sari of yellow gauze silk; jewelry includes necklace, bracelet and earrings. The sari is the chief garment of Hindu women. It is one long piece of cloth wrapped around the waist to cover legs and draped over bosom, left shoulder, and sometimes the head. **Man from North India:** Long tunic-type coat; with tight pants; pointed shoes; no hat. **Hindu Lady with Red Dot on Forehead:** Simple long white skirt; green print blouse; gold necklace and bracelet; sandals on feet. **MARKS:** None on the dolls. *Carlton Brown Collection.*

124

#124. Indian Military Band: 6in (15cm); carved, painted wood; most of them play different types of horns; drummer on far left; two center dolls are directors; 1970s. This wooden type doll continues to be made and can be purchased in the U.S. and other countries at Indian art doll stores. **MARKS:** "Made in India" label on bottom of stand; "Band Pary with Hat" label on box.

#125. Buddhist Sadhu (Holy Man): 11in (28cm); stiffened cloth body and head; painted face with three white lines on forehead; black wavy wool hair down to middle of back; long wool beard, painted mustache; orange linen Buddhist monk attire draped around his body over pants; carries walking stick and wooden bucket to receive alms. *Beverly Findlay Collection.* **MARKS:** "Made in India//Sadhu//Rs...As."

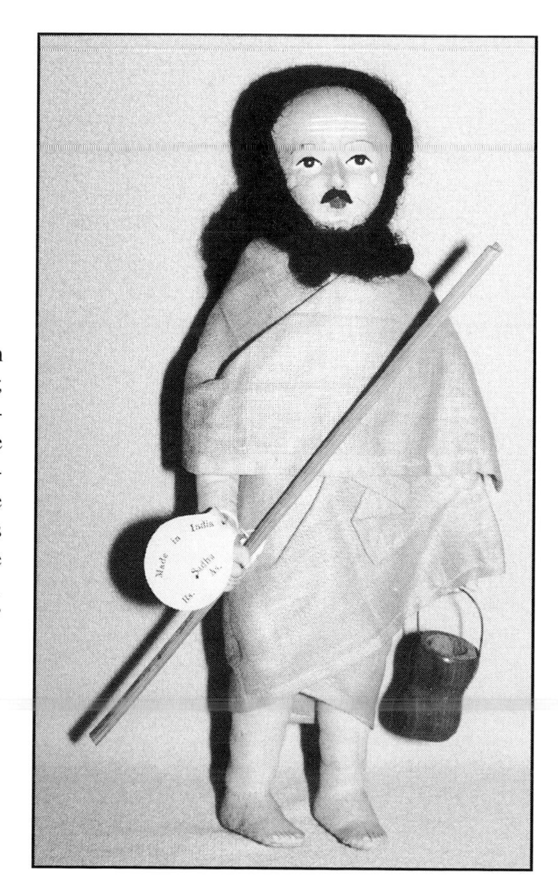

125

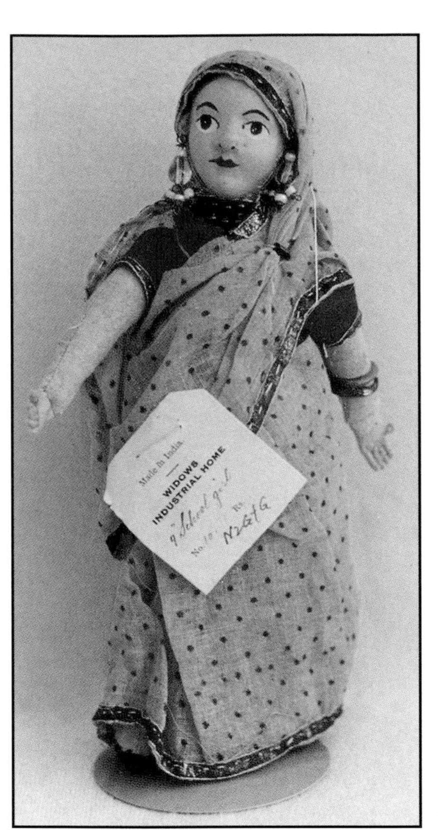

126

#126. School Girl: 9in (23cm); cloth; yellow sari with black dots; rose blouse; jet beads; earrings. *Mary Tanner Collection.* **MARKS:** "Made in India//Widows Industrial Home//School Girl" tag on doll.

#127. ***LEFT to RIGHT:*** **North Indian Antique Style Horse and Rider:** 9.5in (24cm) tall and 8.5in (22cm) wide; painted wood. Since the Mogul days of the 17th century, skilled North Indian artisans have been making these decorative pieces in their family tradition. This version looks old with small cracks and aged looking finish. They are close copies of those museum originals made by craftsmen trained in the time-honored way of those who made the museum pieces; 1990s. **MARKS:** None. Sold by Brimful House Incorporated, Boynton Beach, Florida. **Villager:** Indian Man; cloth over armature; dressed in traditional white, cotton Indian shirt and dhoti pants. **MARKS:** "Villager//Made in India."

127

#128. ***LEFT to RIGHT:*** **Puppet:** 18in (46cm); carved wood head; painted white with red mouth, dots around eyes, and spot on forehead indicating it is a Hindu; stuffed cloth arms; wooden extension of neck which is held by the puppeteer; soft, finely woven beige, red, orange, green print skirt; black jumper with gold trim over skirt; 20th century. **MARKS:** None. **Puppet:** 20in (51cm); carved wood head; red and white headdress; green print cloth body; yellow blouse over wooden extension of neck which is held by the puppeteer; gold ribbon across the chest; black silk skirt; black outlining of facial features; red spot on forehead indicating it is a Hindu puppet; 19th century. These puppets have two purposes: to teach children the Hindu religion as well as to provide a plaything. **MARKS:** "India" museum tag.

128

#129. ***LEFT to RIGHT:*** **Ayah:** 10in (25cm); mask over tan cloth face; burlap body; black real hair in long pigtail down the back; white cotton sari; intricate jewelry in center of hair; wire earrings and nose ring with square gold medallions; bead armlets; bracelets; black leather hand-sewn shoes. **Child:** 4in (10cm); real brown hair; white mask face; burlap body; beautiful pink pleated dress trimmed with lace; gold bracelets. Bharatpur is from Rajasthan State near the city of Delhi. **MARKS:** C.M/S. Mission//Bharatpur//Rajaputana//Ayah and Child" tag sewn on dress of Ayah.
Sandra Strater Collection.

129

130

#130. Indian Man and Woman Puppets: 9.5in (24cm); composition heads; red, yellow, blue, white inexpensive cheesecloth-type Indian robes; 1930s. These are probably inexpensively-made puppets, but they are very colorful characters in the Indian tradition. The expressions of the actors are very important, and the doll artist painted the "feelings" that they were trying to express very well. *Sandra Strater Collection.*
MARKS: None.

131

#131. Sikh Woman: 9.5in (24cm); cloth over armature; black hair; painted face; peach clothes; 1960s. A paper sewn to the back of her costume says, "The Sikh Woman wears a Salvar (a baggy loose pajama), a Kamiz (a shirt-like apparel) and a thin cloth which covers her shoulders and upper chest. Its ends are thrown over the shoulders at the back. She has a pearl and red bead necklace; red and gold bracelets; painted red finger and toenails; and pearl earrings." A man doll originally came with the woman. **MARKS:** (Very hard to read) "Stree Seva Mandir Neighborhood House//siddeshwar Peth, Sholapur// Maharastra, India."

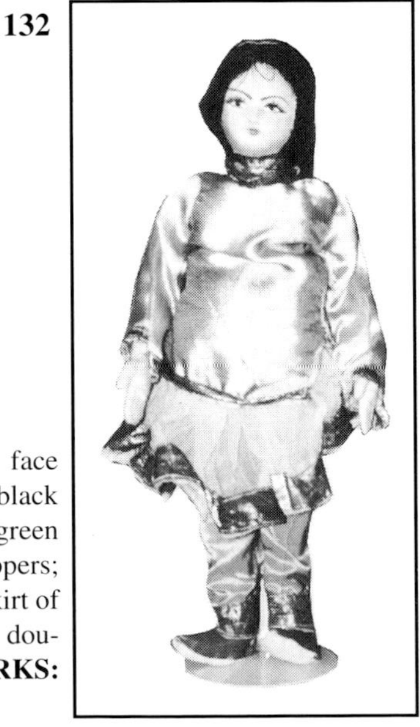

132

#132. Kashmir Doll: 12in (31cm); cloth doll; molded masque face and painted facial features; stitching to indicate fingers in hand; black thread hair styled in two braids; dressed in long-sleeved mint green tunic top and narrow pants with gold trim; coral red satin slippers; "beanie-type" hat; under tunic and over pants is a full gathered skirt of light gray nylon-like fabric edged in the same gold trim as pants; double strand of beads sewn to tunic top. *Sue Ring Collection.* **MARKS:** "Kashmiri" printed on paper stitched to back of costume.

#133. ***LEFT to RIGHT:*** **Hindu Saraswati Goddess of Learning, Wealth, and Good Fortune:** 10in (25cm); royal blue sari with gold trim; all-cloth doll; delicately painted face; four arms; black wig down to hips in back; pearl headdress; tiny pearl necklace; green and gold bracelets; 1960s. Saraswati has four hands. In the first two hands she holds a musical instrument called "veena" (similar to violin). In one of the hands she holds a book, and the remaining hand holds a prayer bead (kind of rosary). With the veena and book, she is the source of learning. **MARKS:** Paper with the above information. **Indian Man:** 13in (33cm); cloth head and body; nicely painted face; leather shoes hand sewn with buttonhole stitch; wearing green gauze turban embroidered with gold thread. Jeweled pin in center of turban; men in the state of Rajasthan often wear this type of turban; orange tunic with purple and silver trim; gold belt; gold necklace with pearls; wears a white dhoti. The dhoti, worn by men especially in the eastern state of Bengal, is a long, wide length of white cotton wrapped around the waist with the end pulled up and tucked between the legs. This is an especially nice doll from India with careful attention to details. **MARKS:** "M. JEWELL" on bottom of right foot.

133

#134. ***LEFT to RIGHT:*** **Malan Woman:** 11.5in (29cm); all cloth; carries basket on her head; green sari over red and blue checked blouse; sari material also used as scarf for head; bracelets on her wrists; 1960s. **MARKS:** "Hand Made India//Malan 11 RS.A.S." **Snake Charmer Kneeling:** 8in (20cm); playing Indian flute-like instrument; blue vest; red print turban; plastic snake between two baskets; 1960s. **MARKS:** "SERRV// India//36904."

134

135

#135. Kerala Dancer: 9in (23cm); clay head and limbs; red dot on forehead; clay head and print blouse; gold necklace; blue, red, and silver hat; blue and silver costume; top; simple white skirt with red trim; bright red panel down the front trimmed with gold decorations; black fur on both sides of skirt bottom; 1980. *Carlton Brown Collection.* **MARKS:** None.

136

#136. ***LEFT to RIGHT:*** **Sikh with Drum:** 10in (25cm); molded baked clay face; cloth body; painted face with mustache; red turban, perhaps from Rajasthan; short black bolero-type jacket with silver trim; long shirt split slightly on each side; puttee-type pants; brown sandals; carrying a drum; 1960s. *Gigi Williams Collection.* **MARKS:** None on doll. **Dhokra Lost Wax Brass Lying Mother and Child:** 4in (10cm). There are only two places in the world, West Africa and India, where the artistic tradition of lost wax metal work is done. Lost wax pieces are made by modeling the form in wax. A mold is then built around the form, and molten metal is poured into the mold. The wax melts off. When the metal cools, the mold is broken to remove the form and thus no two pieces are ever exactly alike. Some of the Indian pieces are known as temple toys because they are found as votive offerings in Hindu Temples. *Brimful House Inc., Boynton, Florida.* **MARKS:** None. **Pathan Sikh From the Northern Frontier:** 11.5in (29cm); all cloth; painted face with mustache and black dot on chin; black hair; turban is high because Sikhs do not cut their hair; wears white trousers, colorful long jacket with green, satin overvest trimmed with silver braid; black and white shirt with cuffs; turban is orange on top with white and turquoise light cotton band wound around the head and tucked into one side of band over the right ear; October 21, 1963. Sold by Kimport who reported that he carried a long walking stick with a round knob at one end which is missing. **MARKS:** "Hand Made, India//Pathan//RS AS."

INDONESIA

Indonesia is an archipelago including Sumatra, Java, the Nusa Tenggara group (which includes Bali), Kalimantan, part of Borneo, Sulawese, Maluku, Irian Barat, and part of New Guinea. There are 3,000 smaller heavily populated islands. Only China, India, Russia, and the United States have a larger population than the Indonesian islands which has 25 languages and 250 spoken dialects.

The clothes of the population range from the type of modern clothes worn world-wide to grass skirts worn on the island of New Guinea. The most popular costume for both men and women is a long wrap-around skirt called a "kain" which is made in many colors and designs according to the region. Sometimes it is gathered or pleated in front or wrapped across. Cotton is grown and woven in these islands. The "kebeya" or jacket, on each island is slightly different. Expensive metal thread, to be woven into kains is imported for important occasions.

Indonesia, especially Java, is famous for Batik designs. Batik cloth designs are painted on the cotton in hot wax. After the wax is dry the material is dyed and then the wax is boiled out of the cloth leaving the design.

In Bali, a colored sah is worn around the waist over the "kebeya". The women wear umbrella shaped bamboo hats when working in the fields. The men wear a "kain" with a white shirt and loose jacket in a variety of colors. Baggy trousers are worn in Sumatra.

Headgear varies and often denotes rank or region. A chief of a village may tie his turban in a special way. The turban on Bali men is knotted in front. Men on some islands wear straw hats or the black hat or pitji. Men are mostly barefoot unless they wear Western clothing.

#137. Indonesia Goddess: 7in (18cm); intricate carved wood Goddess of Hindu religion. This Goddess is especially revered in Bali, a province of Indonesia; 1950s. **MARKS:** "Indonesia:" on bottom of head.

137

#138. Wajang Woman Puppet: 25in (64cm); wood body; gilded with gold; beautiful Javanese skirt with intricate design and colors, beaded girdle. This is a slightly different type of puppet and may not have been used as a shadow puppet. Although puppets seem to have originated in Java, this type of entertainment spread to Siam, Bali, Lombok, the Malay States, Sumatara and surrounding mainland countries. By the 12th century they even appeared in Persia and then migrated to Egypt and other parts of the Muslim world. *Shirley Karaba Collection.* **MARKS:** None.

138

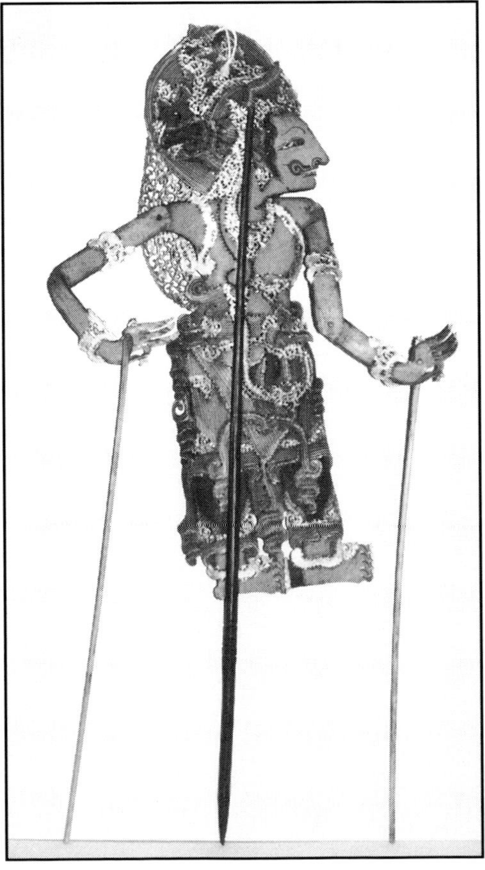

#139. Wajang Figure (Shadow Puppet): 22.5in (54cm); decorated buffalo hide. Shadow show entertainment has existed since the 11th century. The plays generally had religious themes and followed a tradition. The puppets were shown through a screen with the puppeteer working oil-lamps over his head. Usually only one man told the story and operated the puppets, but there could be a bell orchestra of 20 to 25 men accompanying him. There also could be a jester to make people laugh. The plays were lengthy, often lasting all night. Originally these plays were for men only, but when women were allowed to see them, they sat on the side of the showman. Eventually for their entertainment, the puppets were painted and gilded as we see them today. *Shirley Karaba Collection.*
MARKS: None.

139

140

#140. Balinese Rod and Shadow Puppets: 7in (18cm); wooden hand carved; painted heads; wooden arms; clothes over stick which is held by puppeteer; 1994. This set depicts the heroic characters *Krisna, Bima, and Arjuna* from the Hindu epic play *Mahabharata.* Each puppet wears a colorful handsewn cotton batik costume. **(Left to Right):** Purple, white beige print dress; black, embroidered apron and purple ribbons hanging down the sides; black red white headdress. Dark blue with colored flowers print dress; red embroidered apron with red ribbons hanging down side; yellow and red headdress. Yellow, red, black print dress with black embroidered apron and ribbons hanging down sides; black, yellow, red headdress. **MARKS:** None on doll.

#141. Bridal Couple: 5in (13cm) sitting position on cushions; cloth body; papier mâché head; the bride and groom both wear costumes made of white and gold brocade. The bride wears a beautiful lace shawl; the man wears a light pink turban on his head. **MARKS:** None.

141

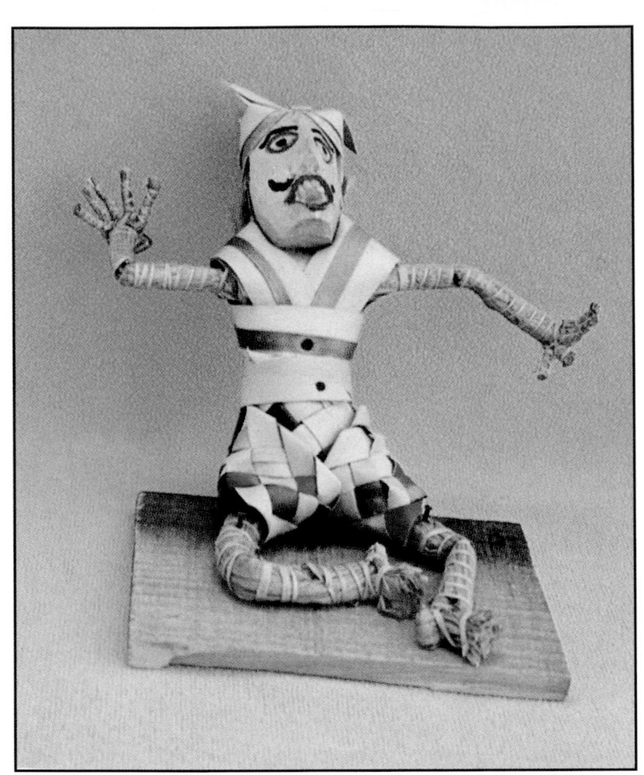

142

#142. Witch Doctor in Sitting Position: 6in (15cm); natural colored and painted palm wood body and clothing; pants are woven with natural, pink, green, purple palm wood; top of clothing is formed with strips of natural and painted gray stripes glued on top; the head is carved from wood; open mouth with carved teeth; painted facial features; headdress made with strips of palm wood with natural hair attached. **MARKS:** None.

143

#143. Balinese Votive Doll: 12in (31cm); made of dried palm leaves; originally used to honor the Rice Mother and pray for a good harvest; thread is used to make the decorations. The plaiting and shaping are done as they sit and sing and take their turn at native dances. It is also a sacrificial doll. **MARKS:** None.

IRAN

The fabled land of Persia, now called Iran, is situated among the mountains and plateaus of the Middle East. Its civilzation dates back to Biblical times. The Arabs conquest introduced Islam, and today the majority of the people are devout Muslims, but they follow the Shiism version and retain their own Farsi language.

The discovery of oil made Iran a wealthy nation. The Shah tried to introduced them to the modern world, but the religious leaders were unhappy and in 1979 revolted and won the war. They are now known as the Islamic-Republic of Iran ruled by religious leaders.

Iran is in southwest Asia bordering Iraq, Turkey, Afghanistan, Pakistan, Russia, Caspian Sea, and the Gulf of Oman. It is the 16th largest country in the world and more than twice the size of Texas.

All Iranians have a strong sense of family and clan regardless of their ethnic background. Ethnic groups include Kurds, Arabs, Baluchis, Jews, Ghulat and others.

The Qasha women wear traditional costumes of old Persia during festivities. The Kurds wear long colorful cotton-type dresses with a shawl headdress. The nomadic men wear shirts and tapered pants. Some Iranian women still wear the "Chador", a cloth that covers the body, hands, legs, and face. In recent years women were pushed out of the workplace and forced into part-time work so nothing hinders their holy duty of motherhood.

#144. Iranian Soldier: 10in (25cm); leather body; nicely painted face; brown beard and mustache; white cotton tunic with high neck; light brown coat with hood; white cotton pants; leather fringed pouch; leather high boots; leather bullet belt; black gun; excellent quality doll. **MARKS:** None.

144

IRAQ

Part of what is known geographically as the Middle East is the country of Iraq. This is another country that has had many different peoples inhabit it for thousands of years. Sumerian, Assyrian, Babylonian, and Chalean cultures have flourished at various times in history.

In the seventh century the Arabs conquered Iraq and brought it under Islamic control. Both main Islam sects the Sunnis and the Shiites live here as welll as Kurds, another Islamic minority. Situated between the Tigris and Euphrates, they prospered as they began to irrigate and control flooding.

When they came under British control, Iraq's source of wealth was petroleum, but a major war with Iran in the 1980's destroyed many of those facilities.

The people are about 75% Arab, the Kurds 20%, and Turkomans, Assyrians, Armenians, and Iranians also live in Iraq.

Although the male population shares the Islamic view that women should be homemakers, many women were needed during the long war with Iran. Most of the women in the cities are not in Purdah. Many of them are now holding jobs.

The Bedouin Arabs are desert wanderers living in woven tents. The Madan Arabs live in the swamplands and are fishermen. The Kurds are semi-nomads who farm and herd livestock to make a living.

The majority of Iraqis speak Arabic.

#145. ***LEFT to RIGHT:*** **Kurdish Woman:** 8.5in (22cm); cloth head and padded wire armature; embroidered facial features; black chiffon Purdah veil; black rayon cloak over blue and white patterned dress; red sash. **Kurdish Man:** 9in (23cm); cloth head; embroidered facial features; black rayon suit with wide maroon waist band; white shirt; 1960s-1970s. **MARKS:** "Iraq//Kurdish (Erbil)" on bottom of stand; "SERRV// Iraq" tag attached to dolls. *Beverly Findlay Collection.*

145

ISRAEL

The roots of today's Israel were born in the mind of Theodor Herzl and the hearts of the Russian Jews. He started and organized a Zionist Congress in 1897. The movement grew. World War I provided the opportunity for the Zionists to promote their goals when Great Britain succeeded in liberating the Middle East from Turkey. The Balfour Declaration expressed support of a Jewish national home in Palestine. The new League of Nations gave the mandate to work toward the Balfour pledge.

The Jews began to come to this poverty-stricken spot where ancient forests had been cut down, sand dunes piled up along the shore and backed up to mosquito filled marshes. They drained the swamps, prepared the soil, planted trees, purchased farms from the Arabs, trained the immigrants to work the land, organized cooperatives and created a new country.

Today arts are everywhere, music, sculpture, and painting, as well as doll art. The Israelis are eager to remember their culture and folk customs, and the pictured dolls reflect the old and the new. Tourists of all religions have made journeys to this new/old land, and they have brought home dolls. The two Brides of Bethlehem *(see page 92, top)* are an example of the beautiful dolls available. Other dolls reflect the religion, the hard time in the Kibbutzim, the women who are police and in the army. Some reflect the joy of festival days. There are also dolls for children to help them understand the struggle. Like the older nations of the world, the Jewish people are already trying to preserve their new heritage through dolls.

#146. *LEFT to RIGHT:* **Lady Carrying a Large Jar:** 7in (18cm); clay head; wire armature body; carrying a large clay jar; orange blouse; purple wrap-around dress and scarf; 1960s-1970s. **MARKS:** "Made in Israel" seal on base. **Sabra Fiddler:** 8in (20cm); clay head; tan peaked hat; black suit; turquoise sweater; pigtails on sides of head; wooden fiddle; 1960s-1970. **MARKS:** "Hand Made by Sabra//Made in Israel" seal on base. *Gigi Williams Collection.*

146

147

#147. ***LEFT to RIGHT:*** **Muslim Bride of Bethlehem:** 11.5in (29cm); all cloth; beautifully painted cloth face; reddish-brown thread hair; wears Khurkah Bethlehem dress of blue rayon with pink cotton embroidered inserts on each side of skirt; at top of dress is an orange cloth panel heavily embroidered with a beautiful flower in gold; blue print belt; red short sleeved jacket with gold trim, blue, pink and gold embroidery; the white veil or Tarboosh indicates she is a married woman; dowry money is on the Tarboosh and on a necklace; imported to the U.S. in 1956 by Kimport. *Doll Talk* says, "This is the elaborately dressed Bethlehem Bride. Every Christmas would not be too often to suggest this all hand-made cloth doll really comes from Manger Square. There is a matching bridegroom." **MARKS:** None on doll. **Strobel & Wilken or Walther & Sohn Muslim Bride of Bethlehem:** 10in (25cm); bisque head, dark sleep eyes; open mouth with teeth; rosy cheeks; bisque legs and arms; composition body; mohair wig; wears a Khurkah Bethlehem dress of dark red striped heavy cotton with green side panels with same type of embroidery as other doll; dark blue short jacket with detailed embroidery around arms and down the front of the jacket; same type of orange panel embroidered with big flower; Tarboosh with white veil; richer bride with more money on Tarboosh and necklace; 1920s. An excellent example of a German doll sent to another country to be redressed. Underneath her bride costume she was already fully dressed with her original German orange chemise.
MARKS: "Crown above Intertwined S & W" on back of head.

148

#148. Jacob from Jerusalem, Israel: 7in (18cm); long tunic called a caftan; black hat bordered with real fur called a "streimel"; carries the Torah which contains the Jewish laws; dressed in "Hassidic" tradition. His letter tells about his schooling, the Hebrew language which has its own alphabet and reads from right to left. He mentions that Israel is even smaller than Massachusetts, but people come from all over the world to live there together. They love music and dancing, especially the "Hora." He is a Sabra which means I was born in Israel. Jacob is a World-Wide Doll Club doll. Today these dolls are attracting much attention for their bright clothes, hidden surprises, and letters which tell about the costuming, history and geography of the country in which the doll was crafted. Each set from a country had a man or woman, girl or boy. His partner is Naomi from Yemen *(see page 162).* **MARKS:** None on doll.

149

#149. Tzora: 9.5in (24cm); toy made of plastic; clothing was all new materials consisting of synthetic wool felt; polyester filling; 1982. *Thelma Purvis Collection.* **MARKS:** "Made in Israel on Kibbutz Tzora."

150

#150. Hassidic Rabbi Carrying the Torah: 7.5in (19cm); wearing fur hat; prayer shawl; 1980s. *Thelma Purvis Collection.*

151

#151. Man from Palestine: 14.5in (37cm); bisque head; cloth body; black hair and beard; red, gold, green cloths with extensive embroidery; purchased in the Holy Land by the original owner in 1920. An example of a Armand Marseille doll sent to Palestine and dressed by hand in the clothes of that country. *Amy Miller Collection.*
MARKS: "390 A.M."

152

#152. ***LEFT to RIGHT:*** **Hassidic Jew of Gur Community:** 7.5in (19cm); modern composition head; mustache; dressed in black belted kaftan and pants; fur hat; 1970s. **MARKS:** "Sabra Made in Israel" seal on bottom of stand. **Sabra (Settler of the New Jewish Territories):** 6.5in (17cm); waxy lightweight vinyl body; black dress; black pants with yellow, blue, red thread trim; red head scarf with white and black embroidery and silver thread woven into the fabric; 1960s. **MARKS:** None (but it was brought to the U.S. by a visitor to Jerusalem.) **Israeli Dancer:** 6.5in (17cm); hard vinyl body; nicely painted face; navy blue print dress with blue, orange, yellow flowers; gold trim at bottom of dress; metallic trim on front of dress and on cuffs of sleeves; white cotton cape; 1960s. The settlers worked hard, but they enjoyed festivals, music and dancing; 1960s. **MARKS:** None. **Woman Member of the Armed Forces of Israel:** 7in (18cm); hard vinyl body; blue woman's uniform; white shirt with blue tie; white and blue military hat. The young women as well as the young men are required by law to spend time in military service; 1960s. **MARKS:** None. **Orthodox Jewish Man:** 6in (15cm) painted wood body and head; white cotton robes with blue lines around bottom of robe; black shirt and pants under robe; fur hat; mustache and beard. **MARKS:** "Hand Crafted, No. Jacob; Made in Israel."

JAPAN

Japanese Doll History

With a long tradition of men and women making dolls both as a hobby and business, it is no surprise that dolls are considered an art form readily collected. Japanese men have been interested in and collecting Japanese dolls since 500 A.D. The women also enjoy doll collecting, especially for the Girls' Day display.

The Japanese doll collector hungers for doll information in order to enjoy his collection. Dolls explain the Japanese way of life and their philosophy.

Types of Japanese Dolls

1. Primitive figures of baked clay, called Dogu, have been found as early as 5000 B.C.
2. By 250-552 A.D. clay figures called Haniwa resembled humans.
3. The tall, slim figures made of folder paper called Anesama have been made since the 8th century.
4. By the 14th-15th century the Hoko had painted features, possible wooden heads, and fabric was used for stuffing and crude clothing.
5. The Tachibina (pair) differentiated between men and women in the late 15th century. Crushed oyster shells (gofum), gold paper, and textiles helped them look somewhat like dolls today.
6. The beloved Gosho emerged in the 17th century and began to look like baby boys of today. Pulverized wood emerged as a material for dolls, and angular dolls mimicked the Noh Actors and other human forms.
7. By the 18th century the Japanese doll makers became quite skillful. The Jui, and the Kamo were much more natural and human. The Saga dolls even had some moveable heads and tongues. The roly-poly Daruma was an innovation. By the middle of this century, real dolls, as we know them today, began to be made in China. They called them Ichimatsu.

8. At the beginning of the 19th century the tubular Kokeshi was invented. They became both play and tourist dolls. The small Izumeka looks like a pin cushion, but it mimicked the babies of farmers who kept them safely in baskets as they worked.

There are examples of many of these dolls in this book, and the authors hope that the dolls in these few pages will encourage collectors to study more about the unusual dolls from Japan that are part of the Japanese everyday life, art, and philosophy.

DEFINITION OF GOFUM

Gofum is scrapings from the shell of a Gofum oyster, ground into a fine powder and mixed with glue from Nikawa seaweed. This mixture is painted over a wood pulp composition face or other body parts many, many times. The number of coats determines the quality of the doll. If the doll has a gofum covered face, it is much more valuable than the modern hard plastic heads of dolls now being made in Japan. One way to determine if gofum has been used is to gently see if there is a small hole where the hair is inserted in the head.

This section features dolls from:

- Girl's Day Festival, March 3rd, pages 97 through 99
- Boy's Day Festival, May 5th, pages 100 through 102
- Noh plays and Noh actors, pages 108 through 110

Girl's Doll Festival
March 3rd

#153. A picture of a later, but still very old, Girl Festival scene. Started in 1910 in Japan, it has more tiers for miniature furniture and other ornaments. The placement of the gofum dolls is the same. *Yoshiko Baker Collection.* *(See earlier scene on page 98.)*
MARKS: None.

153

#154. ***LEFT to RIGHT:* Ichimatsu Ningyo (Girl's Day Doll):** 11in (28cm); gofum face; black hair; pink kimono with white flowers; yellow obi with white lines; 1920-1930. **MARKS:** None. **Tiger:** 7in (18cm) tall; 18in (46cm) long; papier mâché body; nodder head; 1900-1920. The tiger belonged to the mother of the present owner. The tiger is one of twelve animals used for naming the cycle of Japanese years. The year of the Tiger comes after the Year of the Cow; 1910-1920. **MARKS:** None.
Yoshiko Baker Collection.

*Ningyo is the Japanese word for doll.

154

155

#155.

Ancient Japanese people believed that January 1, March 3, July 7, and September 9 were festive days because they could purify themselves and drive out misfortunes at that time. The most important day became March 3. They made paper doll fetishes as part of the celebration and threw them into rivers after the purification ceremony was over. This was the beginning of the present Girls' Doll Festival.

In early Japan the Hina doll represented the aristocracy. By the 15th century the nobles where exchanging gifts of both dolls and doll furniture, and these dolls were kept instead of throwing them in the waters. Gradually the custom evolved into the tiered stand with its rigid placement of dolls. Baby girls often received the basic stand on the first March 3 after their birth. The day was celebrated in the household from that time on. As the years passed, other ornaments were added.

During the Edo period, the custom became very elaborate. Miniature furniture, food, sake, and other period artifacts were added to the scene, but not necessarily on the stand, itself. The Edo period had a slightly different scheme of arranging the various figures, but the placement now used followed this pattern:

Top Tier: the Emperor holding a wooden scepter and Empress wearing 12 kimonos occupy the top tier (dairi-bina dolls). **Second Tier:** ladies in waiting; two standing and one sitting, or two sitting and one standing; dressed in traditional red and white; two outer dolls are provided with hand tables by their side to hold the sake (blue spots in picture). **Third Tier:** five musicians representing the Noh musicians. The singer is from the Noh chorus. (From left to right) A flute player, a singer, a small hand drum player, and ordinary hand drum player, and a big hand drum player. **Lower Tier** holds the zuishin (attendants) who serve the court nobles. On the extreme sides of the lower tier are boxes that hold flowers.

156

#156. Harukoma Doll with Horse: 21in (53cm); silk cloth mask; painted face which looks like gofum; padded cloth body over armature; white brocade blouse under kimono; multi-colored silk kimono lined with red and white print; black and gold ober; right sleeve and lower skirt made from white silk with tiny gold dots; carries a white cloth horse's head with orange fringe hanging down; made by Yoshiko Baker, Japanese doll artist, 1970s. A Kubucki Dancer doll, she is displayed with ceremonial pieces. **MARKS:** None.

Boy's Day Festival, May 5 – Tango no Sekku

Like the Girl's Day Festival, Boy's Day, also called the Festival of Shobu (isris or flag flowers), began in antiquity. Flowers was considered to be a charm against misfortunes in the Japanese Middle Ages. A bath was prepared with plant leaves to keep evil spirits away. The custom is still practiced in some places. Gradually the custom shifted to a towel twisted around a boy's head and a shobu leaf stuck in the front as an ornament. Of course, boys being boys, they gradually started to play soldiers and used the leaf as a sword. Eventually the leaf sword turned into a wooden sword.

About the time the girls were celebrating their day, the Samurai warriors of the Edo period began to build a little palisade outside the gate of their houses with banners, streamers, helmets, spears, and halberds to celebrate May 5. The banners (nobori) turned into the carp, fierce Shoki or Devil Chastiesers and soon the Samurai and townsfolk blessed with boy babies followed the custom of a celebration for the baby boy's first birthday.

By the end of the Edo period the decorations moved into the house, and miniatures looked like a battle camp. The boy dolls became representations of historical or legendary figures noted for daring deeds including the Shoki who had the power of subjugating Devils and other evil. Food for the holiday developed. One custom was two kinds of rice cakes and other food be displayed as an offering. Boy's Day had become a national holiday.

#157. Boy's Day Doll: 10in (25cm); gofum face and arms; inset enameled eyes; two teeth sculptured into mouth; wood body; silk gray pants and kimono top with pictures of cormorant bird woven into the silk. This bird is trained to catch fish *(see page 116, top left)*; red brocade top; pleated beige collar; yellow painted shoes; silver and black striped hat with red silk "rising sun" sewn on tall hat; 19__. *Sandra Strater Collection.* **MARKS:** None.

157

#158. ***LEFT to RIGHT:*** **Boy's Day Doll Samurai Warrior;** 11in (28cm); gofum head, blue painted hands and shoes; shown in full regalia; red Japanese armor; quiver and arrows; sword; gold and red hat; impassive face of true Samurai; 1890-1920. **MARKS:** None. **Lady Musician:** 13.5in (34cm); gofum head and hands; yellow, red, black kimono; red skirt and binding on sleeves; swirled straw hat; Japanese *Zori* on her feet; plays a kakeju, a one-stringed instrument; 1970. **MARKS:** None on dolls.
Sandy Strater Collection.

158

#159. Boy's Day Festival Doll Emperor Jinmu (First Emperor): gofum over wood face and hands; wood body; peach print kimono; high leather boots; bow and sheath of arrows carried on his back; holds pole with his symbol – a golden eagle; 1920s-1930s. He was the Emperor in the 1880s. *Yoshiko Baker Collection.* **MARKS:** None.

159

160

#160. General: 12in (31cm); wood head with coats of gofum; carved wood, painted arms and feet; horse hair; straw-filled form under silk brocade costume; cord-threaded gold and leather panels which were used as armor; gold molded paper decorations over breastplate and back (imitating metal); winged hat with metal "U-shaped" decoration; lance held under left arm; white flag with brown and black stripes held in right hand (indicates #1 in Japan). **White Horse:** carved wood covered with flannel; cleverly spotted to represent horse fur; real horse hair over nose; gray nose and boots on legs of horse; elaborate brocade saddle; sides of body covered with red fringe; original wood platform; mid-Meiji period (1868-1912). The white horse is considered the steed of the gods. It is given as offering to the Shinto shrines. Only rich people could afford such an offering, poorer people gave paintings of white horses to ask favors or thank the gods. White is the color of purity in the Shinto religion. **MARKS:** None.

161

#161. ***LEFT to RIGHT:*** **Kabuki Doll with a Long Letter (Azum Madori):** 5in (13cm); cloth face; wood and wire armature; ribbon hair; peach, green, white, patterned kimono; 1972. Purchased at the Buddhist Temple in Oahu, Hawaii. **MARKS:** "Made in Japan" seal on bottom of stand. **Doll with Type of Spindle (Omaiwa):** 6in (15cm); gofum over wood face; tiny inset black glass eyes; black human hair wig with bun covering red hair decoration; hard plastic hands and legs; wood and wire torso; blue print kimono with white and red flowers; end of kimono material has a vivid pink and red print with multi-colored flowers; red and gold brocade obi (sash); 1950s-1960s. Japanese dolls with gofum are considerably more expensive than the hard plastic or cloth dolls. For more information about gofum *(see page 96).* **MARKS:** None. **Dance of the Seven hats (Dojoji):** 5in (13cm); ribbon hair with gold decorations; cloth over armature body; beige brocade kimono with red and gold decorations; gold and silver obi (Japanese-type sash). **MARKS:** None.

#162. ***LEFT to RIGHT:*** **Baby Boy Playing with Toys:** 8in (20cm); gofum head, hands, feet; wood body; slits for inserted brown eyes; silk print kimono with pictures of flowers, trees, gardens; blue and white checked overgarment; playing with toy drum-like toy; red floor cushion; early 1970s. **Paperdoll Toy:** 5in (13cm); cone-shaped boy with red, white, gold brocade; paper face and helmet; bell at the bottom; 1970s. **MARKS:** None.

162

163

#163. Tenjin: 15in (38cm) high including hat; 19in (48cm) wide; wood carved head and hands; fingers over 3in (8cm) long; inset glass eyes; two spots on head; eyebrows, hair and beard are possibly horsehair; stuffed body; papier mâché hat; silver and gold brocade with red kimono design; red silk border on sleeves; 1835-1850. Students pray to Tenjin for success in their studies. *Sandy Strater Collection.* **MARKS:** None.

#164. Japanese Baby with extra Clothes: 10.5in (27cm); gofum over crushed wood head; cloth body; human hair wig; glass eyes; red nose dots; molded open mouth; indented stomach; dressed in white and red kimono; extra kimono on left red with blue, yellow, white print; extra kimono on right yellow, dark red, and white. *Nan-Maire Graham and Lynn Bartol for Mary Jane's Dolls.* **MARKS:** "Nish//N D in diamond//Nishi Co. Ltd//Made in Japan."

164

165

#165. Meiji Bride: 36in (91cm); bride in white; although this style bridal dress is still used in Japan today, it was also very fashionable during the Meiji period of the last century. This is a modern reproduction patented by Nagara River Ukai; Yoshika Baker doll maker. *Yoshiko Baker Collection.* **MARKS:** None.

166

#166. ***LEFT to RIGHT:*** **Ichinatsu Ningyo:** 20in (51cm); gofum over wood head; black hair; glass eyes; red and white kimono; beige obi; long sleeves. **MARKS:** None. **Two Gosho Ningyo:** 3in (8cm); gofum over pulverized wood; unusually good condition for age; painted decorations; 1910-1920.
MARKS: None.
Yoshiko Baker Collection.

167

#167. Mayoke Doll: 8in (20cm); carved from limb of tree; sculpted face and legs; fierce face painted red and black; two pieces of wood for ears; straw hair; 1980s. Purchased at a rest stop on a freeway in Japan, this doll was used in the home to scare away both the evil spirits, robbers, and other unwanted characters. **MARKS:** Japanese figures on front of doll

168

#168. ***LEFT to RIGHT:*** **Dairi-bini Couple: Emperor:** 4in (10cm) in sitting position; gofum head and hands; two black spots on forehead as a sign of nobility; papier mâché body; holds wooden scepter; lavender and gold brocade robe trimmed in red faille; red faille skirt with rectangular embroidered strip down the center; sitting on a white pillow. **Empress:** 4in (10cm) in sitting position; gofum head and hands; two black spots on forehead as sign of nobility; papier mâché body; beige, gold, purple brocade kimono with front panel of red and white faille; carrying a decorated fan; ornate headdress 3in (8cm) high with gold rectangular metal pieces attached to a frai gold metal frame holding many orange and crystal beads; sitting on a red pillow. In Kyoto the Empress should have been placed to the right of the Emperor. In Edo culture the Empress was placed to the left of the Emperor. **Tetami Dais (Throne):** The upper thrones are covered with green silk with red, yellow, white striped brocade; the lower throne is black lacquer with gold design in the front; late 1800s. **MARKS:** None.

NOH PLAYS AND NOH ACTORS

The Noh plays (often spelled "No") originated in Nara at the Kasuga shrine of the Shinto religion. An animistic religion, Shinto holds rituals to placate and petition the divinities and spirits present in nature. It was previously used to educate the illiterate by teaching them that survival depended on natural forces. The Noh play taught them to be friends with natural forces and appease the hostile gods with gifts, music, chants, rituals, amulets, even cheating them by wearing masks. In between the acts were comic acts called *Tyogen.*

The play became a great art form of the literate and Samurai. The actor was clothed and masked to hide identity, and he used postures, gestures, words, movements, and magnificent costumes for meaning. The only possible stage prop was an old pinetree where the spirits lived to point out the animistic origin of the religion. The Noh play is difficult to understand, but its purpose is to give the spectator a pure, aesthetic experience, named *Kyogen.*

NARA DOLLS

The first Nara dolls were tiny, wooden Noh figures decorating the hats of the priests and musicians at the Kasuga shrine. They were made by a technique called itto-fori which meant carving by one cut in sharp angular planes, and painted in strong colors.

169

#169. The Crane and the Tortoise: Tradition has it that the *Crane* lives a 1,000 years and the *Tortoise* 10,000. "May the Gods bless the Emperor with long life" is the sentiment behind this dance, which is also from a "Noh" play. ***LEFT to RIGHT:*** **Crane:** 5in (13cm); gofum head, hands, feet; inserted eyes; multi-colored brocade kimono; red silk pants; long red hair; brass head dress with Crane figure on top; beating a hand drum; 1910-1930. **Tortoise:** 6in (15cm); gofum head, hands, feet; inserted eyes; beige and rust figured brocade kimono; silk beige pants; black hair on head underneath long white hair; brass headdress with figure of tortoise on top; beating a hand drum; 1910-1930. Clay Chinese building and temple around base of figures. **MARKS:** None.

170

#170. Noh Play Figure: 19in (48cm); entirely bamboo except for mask face; doll made from heavy pieces of bamboo; costume made from shaved pieces of bamboo; white long horse hair inset into bamboo on top of head; mask face made of molded, hard plastic; inset painted eyes; inset teeth; white horns set into top of head; 1950. The mask represents one of the evil spirits of nature. **MARKS:** None.

171

#171. ***LEFT to RIGHT:*** **A Hakata-ningyo Representing a Noh Character:** 9.5in (24cm); beautifully decorated fired clay dolls. Hakata, the commercial center of Fukuoka in the north of Japan, has a 350 year history of making bizarre clay Hakata-ningyo dolls. With the decline in clay dolls in the 20th century, they began to create art dolls. Hakata-ningyo dolls are now ornaments rather than folk dolls. Along with actor dolls, they make dancing dolls and other uncommon dolls which portray the modern sand customs. **MARKS:** The actual signature of the maker is on the shoe. The seal of the company is on the bottom of the base. **Ichimatsu Doll:** 8in (20cm); doll is wearing a "furisode," a long-sleeved kimono worn by children and unmarried girls; orange and gold material is woven to scale; gofum face, hands, legs; cloth body stuffed with straw; joints are wired to make them movable; horse hair; inset glass eyes; carrying a "gotenman" (soft ball) which could be used in the house. This is a Girl's Day doll which may have been a gift to add to the decorations for the celebration. **MARKS:** None.

172

#172. ***LEFT to RIGHT:*** **Woman Serving Tea:** 9in (23cm); beige and gold brocade kimono lined with red cloth; gofum head, inset eyes; black mohair with long hair down her back below her knees; black lacquer table with red top; metal bowl and pot on table. 1880-1900. **MARKS:** None. **Noh Actor:** 9in (23cm); gofum head; Noh hat with beige band at bottom; purple and white kimono with hexagon design; puppet can be seen on a black string near the bottom of the kimono on left side; 1920s. **MARKS:** None. *Shirley Karaba Collection.*

173

#173. Lion Dancers: 1.5in (3cm); nicely painted for the size of the body; one with white hair has intricate clothes in shades of blue, white, black; one with red hair is painted with dark green, light blues and white clothing; dolls represent actors dancing the "Lion Dance of Shishimai"; dolls are supposed to represent a shojo or drunkard; available in many sizes. **MARKS:** None.

#174. Gosho-Nigyo Doll: 10.5in (27cm); gofum over pulverized wood; scantily-clad, statue-like baby boy; large head. According to tradition, the doll originated in Kyoto during the Edo period. Nobles surrounding the Emperor contracted for these dolls to give as presents to the daimyo (feudal lords) and the Samurai (warriors). In turn these people brought dolls as presents from their area when they made their journey to Kyoto *(see page 117, top)*. At first the dolls were made of clay, but later made of wood or pulverized wood covered with gofum. The dolls come in many sizes and poses; their costumes are short, usually down to just below their waist; some are very ornate; 1850-1880. **MARKS:** Maker's name in Japanese on the doll's stomach.

174

175

#175. Takeda Doll: 10in (25cm); gofum over wood painted head; carved wood hands and feet; paper stuffing for body; ornate painted ornaments imitating armor used in chest area; 1700s. Takeda dolls were invented by Omi I because of his love for the theatre. Made in dramatic poses with hand painted faces, upturned eyes and down turned mouths, their costumes were mostly orange and green woven textiles over paper base for kimonos and pantaloons.
MARKS: None

176

#176. Hagoita (New Year's Doll): 18.5in (47cm) Japanese lady; decorated piece of wood shaped like a paddle; red, white, gold, brocade dress and hairpiece; corduroy-type material used for hair; silver hair decorations; 1980s. This is an indoor/outdoor game similar to badminton which is played at New Year's time. A twisted paper flower is batted back and forth. *Sandra Strater Collection.*
MARKS: "15A and Japanese writing" on box.

#177. Musician Sakura-ningyo (Cherry Doll): 11in (28cm); stiffened fabric face mask; entire body is built up on padded wire framework; hair styled in three buns; flowers woven into buns; gold jewelry attached to ribbon in hair; long red brocade lined with white silk; long panel sleeves; black brocade obi sash; vinyl hands and feet; yellow ribbon bow at hipline; carries warrior's gold helmet with long white hair attached; 1982. A "shelf doll," this doll represents the Warrior's Handmaiden in the Kabuki drama. The black lacquer base is a music box, and the base turns as the song is played. **MARKS:** None of the song on bottom of music box.

177

#178. Kabucki Dancers from the Kabucki Theatre *LEFT to RIGHT:* Hanagasa – The Flower Hat Dance: Red brocade kimono and black print obi in back; her large hat is made of flowers. **Yuki – The Snow Dance:** Purple scarf on head; short pink print kimono; black obi; carrying a lavender and black umbrella. **Chiyodajo – Princess:** White print dress; black and silver obi; carrying a hat with a large peach-colored flower. The dolls are all 21in (53cm). **MARKS:** None.
Yoshiko Baker Collection.

178

179

#179. Japanese Squeaker Doll: 10.5in (27cm); gofum face and hands; inset glass eyes; black stiff wig; clay feet and legs to knee which is wired to wooden box with squeaker mechanism that "squeaks" when pressed; red and beige cotton kimono; long sleeves of little girl; red and white ovi; one white collar underneath top of kimono; 1920s into 1930s.

#180. JAL (Japanese Airline) Stewardess Holding a Toy Airplane: 8in (20cm); dark blue uniform; cloth over armature; mask face; late 1960s. This doll was purchased during a flight on the JAL airplane. She was modeled after the BARBIE® Doll. **MARKS:** "J.A.A.//J a 5038"

180

181

#181. Ichinatsu Ningyo: 7.5in (19cm); gofum face and hands; wood body; painted eyes and eyebrows; black horse hair; red and white brocade kimono with blue flowers; white and red print brocade down the front and back; hair pulled up over red cushion on top of head; holding tiny gofum decorated cat in her hands; gofum dog in front. The doll is seated on a black lacquered piece of wood; behind her is a Japanese screen. Purchased in Japan in the early 1980s. **MARKS:** None.

#182. ***LEFT to RIGHT:*** **Fukuruko Represents Wisdom and Learning:** 12in (31cm); gofum over wood head; inset glass eyes, teeth, hair; long ear lobes; long white beard; wrinkles in forehead; hands are unpainted wood; feet are black painted wood; the rest of the body is stuffed newsprint under costume; kimono is made of gray paper with red and gray hand stitching; back of kimono is same gray paper with white, green, and red stitching; wide sleeves lined with gray and beige paper; beige paper belt; purple silk inner collar; beige collar on outside; pre-1900. The longer the earlobes, the richer the Fukuruko. **MARKS:** None. **Japanese Nobleman:** 6.5in (17cm); thin composition face well-molded with excellent detail; black hair, sideburns, mustache; inset glass eyes; wood hands and feet; body stuffed with newspaper or straw; kimono is made of gray or beige paper with red, gray, and brown stitching; sleeves are red cotton tied at wrist; gray brocade short pants; cloth scarf with painted design; red tie; three white collars indicate he is a wealthy man; 1880-1890. *Sandy Strater Collection.* **MARKS:** None.

182

#183. Wrestling Coach: 18in (46cm); silk face; gold brocade kimono; pleated from waist down; made by a Japanese doll artist; 1960s. *Thelma Purvis Collection.* **MARKS:** None.

183

#184. Fisherman with Cormorant Bird: 7in (18cm); hard plastic head, arms, legs; cloth body (man); dark blue hat and shirt; straw skirt. The cormorant bird naturally seeks fish from the water to eat. The fisherman puts a rope around the bird's neck so he cannot swallow the fish, and he was pulled back to the fisherman who takes the fish. The bird is rewarded with some of the fish so he will continue his efforts. **MARKS:** Label seen in picture tells the above story about the bird and fisherman.

184

#185. Musicians Playing a Koto: 5.5in (14cm) x 3in (8cm); figures are wood; painted faces, hair and hat; figure on left is dressed in red brocade with ribbon trim; figure on right has white and gold brocade costume with lavender and white thread at neckline. The painted figure has a Noh actor painted on the back board. **MARKS:** None.

185

186

#186. Tachi-bini Dolls: 8in (20cm) clay dolls with paper clothing. These dolls came in pairs (man and woman), and there are hundreds of different types using a variety of materials. The clothing is usually made of paper, the features and colors are delicate. Often pictures of these dolls were used for screen decorations as can be seen in this picture. The bodies of the men are rectangular at the top. The bodies of the women are usually triangular. The word hina means miniature, often used for the word doll. The most used word for doll is ninyo. *Yoshiko Baker Collection.* **MARKS:** None.

187

#187. Daimyo Gyoretsu (War Lord and High Class Long Line of People): 20in (51cm) x 5in (13cm) red lacquer and glass case; 14 figures including a Princess on a litter, the War Lord on a horse; figures are less than one inch except Princess and War Lord; all figures are wood intricately carved and painted. **MARKS:** None.

#188. Mask-Dance Doll: 7in (18cm); painted hard plastic; Japan's traditional man in ornate gold and silver pants; red, orange turquoise white jacket; 1960s. **Three masks in set (top to bottom):** *Tengum* – long-nose goblin that dances on the stage in Noh-play "Kurma Tengu"; *Hyottoko* – a buffon in "Kagura" who presents a comical dance to invisible Gods at the shrine stage; *Okame* – a woman with ideal personal beauty who dances in front of the gods. Other sets have six masks. The additional characters are: *Kitsune* – a fox known as a possessor of magic power, acting as if it is running errands for gods in "Kagura" play; *Oni* – personification of an evil, sometimes appearing as bandits in "Kagura"; *Saru* – the "monkey" playing a supporting role in "Kagura, a likeness of Sarutahiko, the god of travel. The older sets come in wooden boxes. **MARKS:** "Made in Japan" on right side of box.

188

KOKESHI DOLLS

The simplest of all the Japanese dolls; the bottom is a round cylinder with a sphere-shaped head. The dolls were first made in the late part of the Edo period by the farmers of the Tokhoku region in Northeast Honshu. An area of hot springs, people came to cure their ailments. Soon it became a fashionable spa as it is today. The inhabitants saw another way to make money from the tourists by making *Kokeshi* dolls. Kokeshi dolls are made in many other forms and parts of Japan. There is even a candy shaped like a Kokeshi doll.

189

#189. ***LEFT to RIGHT:*** **Kokeshi Boy Nesting Doll:** 5in (13cm); all wood painted in bright colors. **Boy:** Beige kimono with brown sash; over the kimono is a blue jacket with white decorations; black hat. **Girl:** Dressed in a pink and green kimono decorated with flowers and a bright red jacket with white dots; 1970s. There are four dolls in each "nest" representing children. Their clothing color is similar, but different from that of their parents. **Flashlight Kokeshi Dolls:** 7.5in (19cm); the doll on the left wears an orange flowered, brocade kimono; the doll on the right wears a brown, flowered brocade kimono. These dolls are actual flashlights with batteries. They were purchased at a "sape" in the Tohoku region of Japan by the authors. **MARKS:** None.

#190. Kokeshi: 6in (15cm); unpainted head; white face; loose-jointed head; wood body; no limbs; head turns; red base painted with white flowers; dolls originally made in the Tohoku region of northern Japan; primitive play dolls; now souvenir dolls sold mostly at spas. *Thelma Purvis Collection.* **MARKS:** None.

190

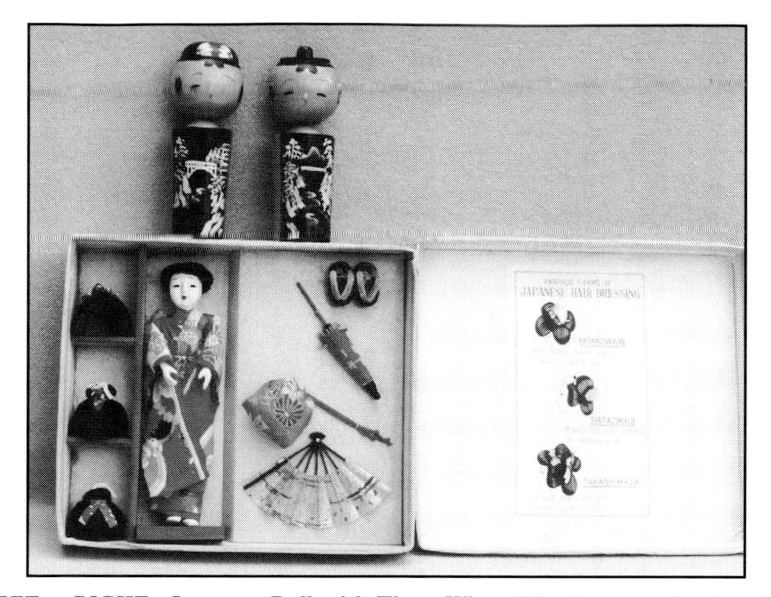

191

#191. ***LEFT to RIGHT:*** **Japanese Doll with Three Wigs:** 6.5in (14cm); painted papier mâché; black wig; traditional red, yellow, green print kimono; obi on back; inset eyes. **Various forms of Japanese Wigs (top to bottom):** Momoware for young teen ages 16-17 years old; Shitajimage mostly for man-actress in Kabuki play; Takashimada for well-matured girls 19-22 years old. Accessories: shoes; umbrella; carrying bag; fan. 1960s. **MARKS:** "JAPAN" on doll's base; "Japanese Doll with Three Wigs" on cover of box; "Hanako Company" on box. **Kokeshi Couple:** all wood; lovely black panel with Japanese scenes painted in white; girl has black hat with red inset with white painted design; other girl has similar scene panel with knob on top. **MARKS:** None. *Sandy Strater Collection.*

#192. Collection of Anesama-ningyo: paper dolls (literally, elder sister) made by folding paper; made in homes and other places as a pastime; patterned (chiyogami) and plain (irogama) paper. This is a chance for Japanese children and ladies to show hairstyles and fashions of all Japanese doll history periods. There are no facial features. *Yoshiko Baker Collection.* **MARKS:** None.

192

193

#193. Mimikaki Doll: 6in (15cm); carved wood body; similar to a Kokeshi doll; black hair with yellow and red flowers; brown and beige kimono; 1980. The head is on a long piece of wood which can be lifted from the body; the end is curved and can be seen through the hole in the bottom of the body. This is an instrument with which people can clean their ears. Also a Japanese souvenir doll. **MARKS:** "MIMIKAKI" in Japanese Writing.

194

#194. ***LEFT to RIGHT:*** **Izumeko Doll:** 3in (8cm); gofum face; papier mâché body; red, white, gold brocade; bow with fringe in front. Today this souvenir-type doll, often mistaken for a pincushion, is brought home by visitors to Japan. **Izumeko Doll:** 3.5in (9cm); gofum face; red and gold brocade quilts; silk red and white clothing on part of doll not under the quilts; very tiny head and eyes that are inset in face; light wicker basket. **Izumeko Doll:** 3.5in (9cm); gofum face and hands; black and yellow print kimono; much larger head for same size doll; large slits for inset eyes; no quilts in basket. These dolls represent the custom of fastening babies in baskets while the parents were working in the fields or around the house. This is an old custom said to be from North Japan. Children played with toys hung on the rims. **MARKS:** None.

195

#195. Early Mitsuore (Triple-Jointed) Doll: 19in (48cm); layers of gofum over carved wood except around upper arms which are cotton wrapped; inset enameled eyes; arched eyebrows; pierced nostrils; open/closed mouth with upper carved teeth; painted short black hair; both front and back of head has slot with a thin cord inserted in slot with wisps of real hair tied to cord; pressed paper removable cap; pressed paper torso with molded nipples; upper cloth arms, lower arms of pressed paper, swivel composition hands; swivel upper legs of pressed paper; jointed at knee lower legs of pressed paper; swivel composition feet; original multi-colored kimono; both male and female dolls are sexed; late Meiji period (1880s-1912). An early example of a play doll probably named after the famous actor of the 1750 era. *Bill Zito Collection.* **MARKS:** None.

THE HASHEMITE KINGDOM OF JORDAN

Today, Jordan is a land of contrasts between the new and the old. Like other older cultures, Jordan treasures its past. Organizations have tried to help refugees by making and selling dolls which reflect the previous life styles. An example is the Y.M.C.A. Centre//Aqabat Jabber Refugee Camp//Jericho//Jordan.

A visitor will see Jordanians dressed in modern clothes. Jeans are allowed – but no shorts. Some Arabs still travel by camel in Bedouin garb, and costumes of the Circassians from Caucasus, and other ethnic groups which have sought refuge are still seen.

The predominate religion is Sunni Muslim. Both men and women of that sect wear an ankle-length, free-flowing cotton gown called a "thawab."

Men sometimes wear a sleeveless cotton, wool, or a camel-hair coat called an "abah." The practical scarf the men wear on their head is a "kaffiyak" which may be a white or checked cloth. It is placed on the head so the middle point hangs in back and the ends hang over the shoulders. It is held in place by a black coil named the "agal." It is excellent protection from sun and sandstorms.

For women , a "kaaftan" – long-sleeved, ankle-length dress, can be plain for daily wear or ornately embroidered with traditional family patterns for formal occasions. The women also wear the "kaffiyak" on their heads, often without the black coil.

196

#196. ***LEFT to RIGHT:*** **Men and Women with Brass Camel in Background; Jordanian Man:** 8in (20cm); composition head; painted features with heavy black lines; jointed, movable arms; red wooden legs; wooden body; wears a embroidered gown called "sthawab"; blue short-sleeved "abah" over coat; bright red sash; "kaffiyak" with "agal" black coil on head; 1950-1960s. **Jordian Woman:** 7.5in (19cm); composition head; painted features with heavy black lines, jointed movable arms; wooden body; wears hand embroidered black "kalaftan" with wide dark red sash; white chiffon veil; matches man; 1960s-1970s. **MARKS:** (Both Dolls); "Jordan" written on wooden feet. **Jordanian Man:** 7.5in (19cm); stockinette face with black embroidered facial features; cloth over armature body; blue and white striped "sthawab" with white belt; black "abah" with gold trim with red balls covered with gold thread; white "kaffiyak" held in place with an "agal." **Jordanian Married Lady:** 8.5in (22cm) with headdress; stockinette face with black embroidered facial features; cloth over armature body; black "kaaftan" with red hand embroidery; red belt with gold trim; high pink "tarbooth" (fez-styled hat) with sequins indicating coins; thin white cotton veil. This headdress indicates she is a married lady; 1950s-1960s. **MARKS:**"WORLD Y.W.C.A. CENTRE//AQABAT JABER REFUGEE CAMP//JERICHO-JORDAN" seal on bottom of wooden stand.

#197. Trans-Jordan Arab Doll in Jerusalem. **Lady:** 6.5in (17cm); embroidered cloth face; cloth padded wire armature; black kaaftan heavily embroidered with red thread; long orange chiffon scarf over her head; carrying a straw basket filled with balls of fruit. **Man:** 7in (18cm); gold and white striped satin thawab; black cloth abah; white fringed kaffiyak; black agal which holds headdress in place. *Gigi Williams Collection.* **MARKS:** "JERUSALEM Dar Al Awlad" seal on stand.

197

#198. Jordan Lady Purchased at Aqaba Bazar: 10.5in (27cm); painted plaster face; heavy black make up around eyes; piece of square wood body with feet nailed on so she can stand; stuffing around upper part of wood; black thread hair; red rayon veil not covering face; blue dress with red machine embroidery; basket of fruit on head; 1970s-1980s. **MARKS:** "aqaba bazar//Made in Jordan" seal on plastic wrapper; also on bottom of feet.

198

199

#199. ***LEFT to RIGHT:*** **Jordanian Woman;** *(see page 121.)* **Jordanian Musician:** 6in (15cm); stockinette face; black embroidered features; wire armature body; striped "sthawab" with black belt; white low Jordanian headdress; holding wooden flute; mid-1970s. **MARKS:** "World Y.M.C.A. Centre//Aqabat Jaber Refugee Camp//Jericho Jordan." on bottom of wooden stand.

KOREA

Korea borders China on the north and is a peninsula east of Japan. The Korean people make and enjoy beautiful dolls. In Korean a doll is a "eenhyong."

The Koreans call their country "Chosun" – the land of the morning calm. They enjoy bright colors in clothing. Music and dancing is important to them.

For special occasions Koreans may still wear the old traditional clothing, and a few rural people wear it everyday. Women wear the *chima* (long skirt) gathered to a bodice and topped by a very short *chogori* (jacket) that is tied on one side by a wide strip of cloth in a single bowknot.

Traditional costume for men is white *bahi*i (long pants). They are topped by a sleeveless vest and covered by a *turumagi* (long coat). This is tied in front with a bow like that on the woman's *chogori.* The men wear a tall hat with a wide brim. The ladies wear a black hat with a high piece on the back of the hat.

200

#200. Korean Missionary Doll: 9in (23cm); all handsewn cloth; excellent painted face; brought back by a missionary from Korea; white long simple cotton dress trimmed in red; 1960s. *Carlton Brown Collection.* **MARKS:** None.

#201. Two Korean Men Dressed for Special Occasions: 9in (23cm); long white (often silk or brocade) coat called a "Torumagi;" traditional black horsehair hat to protect his topknot. This was worn by married men. Unmarried men wore their hair in pigtails and went hatless. *Shirley Karaba Collection.* **MARKS:** None

201

#202. ***LEFT to RIGHT:*** **Korean Woman:** 10.5in (27cm); papier mâché head; cloth body; dressed in traditional Korean clothes; long yellow silk skirt with black cuffs at wrists; matching yellow jacket; wide maroon strip of cloth tied in a single bow knot; black thread hair; carries basket on her head; 1960s. **MARKS:** "Korean Doll//Made in Seoul Korea." **Viet Nam Doll:** 16in (41cm); hard vinyl body; dressed in traditional clothes; hair pulled away from face and wrapped into a bun on top of head; turquoise dress fitted at waist; white rayon long pants hang below dress; gold necklace; red high-heeled shoes; 1960s-1970s. This doll was brought to the U.S. by a soldier during the Viet Nam war. **MARKS:** None. **Korean Young Man:** 8.5in (22cm); papier mâché face; stuffed paper body wrapped with cloth; white brocade calf-length side pants; maroon heavy organdy coat with wide sleeves folded in front; gold painted trim on coat collar; stiffened paper hat with large flaps on each side and gold painted crown design on front of hat. **MARKS:** None.

202

203

#203. ***LEFT to RIGHT:*** **Korean Lady:** 12in (31cm); painted silk mask face; cloth body; white satin top with silky white gauze skirt over green brocade underskirt; red ribbon trim around neck and sleeves; thread hair; flowered wreath around head; mounted on blue stand; purchased at Korean exhibit at the Montreal, Canada exposition in 1967. **MARKS:** None. **Korean Boy and Girl:** 9in (23cm); painted silk mask face with cloth over wire armature body; boy is wearing purple pants and green jacket and carries a basket; multi-colored straw sandals; the girl is in a long pink dress with a basket of flowers; both have multi-colored stripes on their costumes; 1974. **MARKS:** "Made in Korea//Watergate//1974." **Old Korean Man:** 9in (23cm); painted mask face; dark gray heavy thread hair; black stovepipe-type hat made of cloth covered cardboard; long white whiskers; white brocade costume; on blue wooden base; mid-1970s. *Shirley Karaba Collection.* **MARKS:** "From Korea" on base.

Kimport sold an old Korean couple abut 10in (25cm) each. The Man had the same costume, but he held a long gold pipe instead of a cane. The Old Lady had gray hair held in a bun at the back of her neck by a green comb; 1975. (Not Pictured).

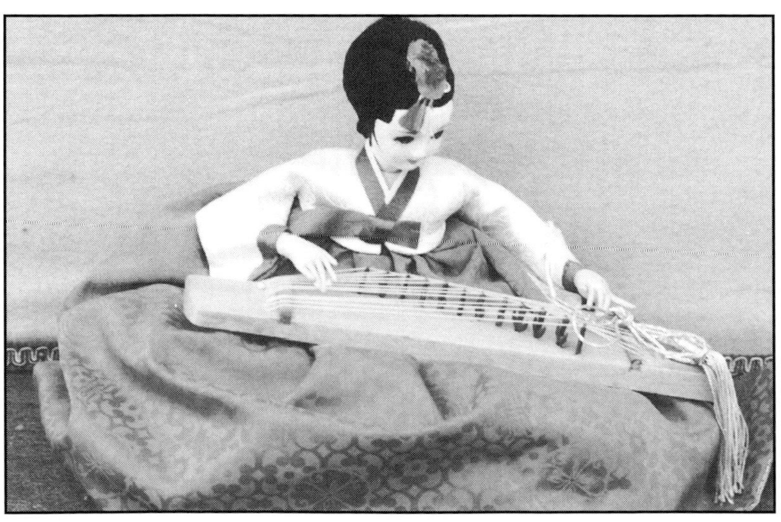

#204. Lady Playing Stringed Korean Instrument: 8in (20cm) in seated position; all cloth; white blouse with red ribbon trim at collar; flower in hair; blue brocade long, full skirt; 1950s. *Carlton Brown Collection.* **MARKS:** "Made in Korea" on bases

204

#205. Lady with a Hand Drum: 9in (23cm); multi-striped blouse; white skirt; 1960s. *Carlton Brown Collection.* **MARKS:** None.

205

206

#206. Korean Lady Dancer: 15in (38cm); cloth doll; all original traditional rose colored robe of Korea. *Thelma Purvis Collection.*
MARKS: "Park's Korean Doll"

#207. Rice Straw Girl: 9.5in (24cm); body is straw over wood; girl carrying flowers; wearing purple ribbons; 1983. *Thelma Purvis Collection.* **MARKS:** "Made in Korea" on base.

207

KUWAIT

Kuwait is a small, oil rich country on the northwest edge of the Persian Gulf. Mostly a desert country with a hot climate, its territory stretches 95 miles east to west and 90 miles from north to south.

The government is a kingdom headed by the ruling al Sabah family. The family indirectly controls the huge oil wealth, and it has created a prosperous, modern welfare state.In spite of helping Iraq with its war against Iran, Iraq invaded Kuwait and created the Persian Gulf War. Kuwait was almost destroyed. With the help of many countries, including the United States, Iraq was overcome. Kuwait has set out to rebuild their nation with oil revenues.

Islam is the religion. Two thirds of the people are Sunni Muslim, but the other third are Shiite Muslim. Some of these families are rich merchant families.

208

#208. Kuwaiti Couple: 7in (18cm); cloth and plastic; lady dressed in dark blue "Kaftan" with embroidered white and light blue panel down the front with matching veil. The man is dressed in a lavender and white striped long sleeved "sthawab"; matching "kaffiyak" (headdress) with "agal" (coil to hold on headdress); collected in 1988 by the Rosalie Whyel Museum of Doll Art. *Rosalie Whyel Museum of Doll Art. Susan Hedrick Photographer.* **MARKS:** None.

LAOS

A small country, Laos is in the mountainous north of the Indochinese Peninsula. It borders China, Cambodia, Vietnam, Burma, and Thailand. As a route for invaders, Laos has been influenced by many different customs.

Called communities, the major people are the Lao Lum, Lao Soung, Hmong, Lao Theung. However, the Lao government counts at least 68 tribal minorities.

Like most of the other countires of the world, simple pullover tops and pants or blue jeans for the men, and simple tops and skirts or pants for the women are gradually becoming the modern dress. However, each of the various groups is trying hard to maintain their own customs and dress, especially during festivals or when visiting friends. There is an effort to teach the young the "old" ways.

#209. Kha Oma Doll in Kneeling Position: 9in (23cm); mask face; cloth over armature; long slender fingers; long black dress and headdress; dress has homespun panel around him; doll has silver neck chains; pendant, ornaments on headdress; earrings; bracelets; 1974. The dolls were made by the Vanida S. Monghkhone Company. **MARKS:** None on doll; pamphlet about the company shown in picture.

209

LEBANON

Lebanon is an ancient land which lies at the end of the eastern Mediterranean Sea. It was once called the land of Canaanites, later known as Phoenicians. Because it is on a major trade route of the world, many people with differing ethnic backgrounds and religions live there.

Still rebuilding from a war between the Christians and the Muslims, the people have many problems to solve. There are large areas of dry land, with two major rivers providing irrigation for farming. The cities and most of the people live near the Mediterranean coast.

The city of Beirut was once one of the most fashionable cities of the world. Tourists flocked to the cosmopolitan life and beaches. Even today some people dress in the latest Paris fashions. Some women are covered head to foot in the Burkas of Islam. These women are among the best educated and working women in the Muslim world.

Lebanon has been at the center of education for centuries. The schools of both religions are known world-wide for their excellence.

210 **211**

#210. Lebanese Man: 10in (25cm); molded clay face; sponge-like body; well painted face with black mustache; yellow rayon shirt; black pants; black belt embroidered with blue thread; brown felt conical fez with black ribbon wrapped around rim; playing musical instrument; 1965. *Gigi Williams Collection.* **MARKS:** "Lebanese" on stand.

#211. ***LEFT to RIGHT:*** **Lady:** 6in (15cm); sculpy-type face; cloth over wire frame body; yellow, green, orange, striped skirt; purple, blue, gray flowered top; long, white, scarf on head; 1960s. **MARKS:** "Made in Lebanon" on wooden base. **Man Beating Drum:** 5.5in (12cm); papier-mâché over armature; yellow shirt; brown pants; black Arab headdress with coil around head; 1960s. **MARKS:** "Made in Lebanon" on base.

MALAYSIA

Malaysia, in south-east Asia, has 13 states including the Federal Territory of Kuala Lumpur, the capital and 11 states from West or Peninsular Malaysia. Sabah and Sarawak belong to Malaysia, but they are on the northern part of the island of Borneo. Pinang and a small section of the mainland form another state.

About 47% are Malay, 33% are Chinese, 9% are Indian and Pakistani, 4% are Dyaks and the rest are from other countires.

Dyak villlages are huge homes, called long houses, in which large family groups live. Many of the inhabitants wear versions of Western clothes. However, some dress as their religion dictates. Batik cloth is an important craft. It is the art of dyeing cloth by using wax to cover areas to be dyed. The wax is then boiled out of the material.

Their theatre arts include Chinese opera and shadow plays called Wayang Kulit.

212

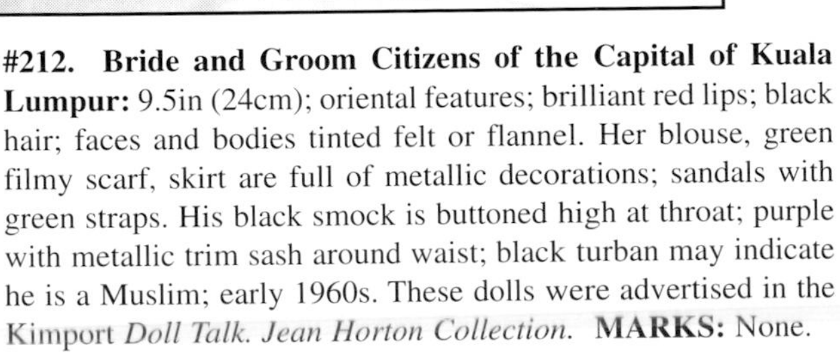

#212. Bride and Groom Citizens of the Capital of Kuala Lumpur: 9.5in (24cm); oriental features; brilliant red lips; black hair; faces and bodies tinted felt or flannel. Her blouse, green filmy scarf, skirt are full of metallic decorations; sandals with green straps. His black smock is buttoned high at throat; purple with metallic trim sash around waist; black turban may indicate he is a Muslim; early 1960s. These dolls were advertised in the Kimport *Doll Talk. Jean Horton Collection.* **MARKS:** None.

213

#213. Malay Lady: 9.5in (24cm); cloth; large eyes with bright blue eye shadow; square headdress with black button in middle; dark blue blouse; black pants; light blue apron; carrying a shopping bag; 1985. **MARKS:** "Gama Supermarket and Department Store" label on base.

MONGOLIA

Mongolia is divided between the northern Mongolian People's Republic and Inner Mongolia, a province of China. Both have similar northern living conditions. The cultural life of Mongolia and that of the people of Tibet is similar. They both believe in Tibetan Buddhism or Lamaism, and they have some similarities in clothing because of their location in the high latitude location.

On Mongolian plains, the traditional clothes for both men and women are dels. These are loose ankle-length robes with high collars buttoned from left to right as it crossed the body. Often they have fur linings to protect them against the cold. Thick pants are worn under the dels with high leather or felt boots. They wear many layers of cloth socks. Originally only the men wore sashes, but now women wear them also. A Mongolian Chinese provincial girl doll is shown with a similar costume *(see page 66, top left)*.

Mongolian men's hats are fur trimmed, and often fur-lined like those in Tibet *(see page 232)*. A lighter-type hat for warmer weather is similar to the Chinese Manderin's hat. A third type of man's hat is a helmet for fighting. Hats are generally trimmed with fur or decorated with feathers at the back. Most hats had a button, spike, or tassel at the top.

Women wear round fur hats under scarfs in the winter.

214

#214. Mongolian Woman: 11in (28cm); clay-like head with painted features; rolled cardboard body; molded cardboard body; no legs; shoes are attached to trousers; big hat has beaded fringe of antique crystal beads; all silk turquoise shirt with orange scarf; purple panels down each side of dark blue trousers; holds a beautiful decorated paddle on wrapped wire which is used as some type of game; 1920s-1930s. *Shirley Karaba Collection.* **MARKS:** None.

NEPAL

Nepal, between India and Tibet, was known as the "Forbidden Land" and few westerners were allowed to enter until 1951. The small villages were separated by rugged mountains, and it took many days to walk from one to another. The people did not speak a common language and lived in tribal groups, Gerkas, Sherpas, etc.

The country is now open to visitors, and is modernizing medicine, education, and some new forms of transportation. However, they try to keep their beautiful culture alive.

Hindus have carved many facades of buildings, made statues, dolls, masks, etc. of stone and wood representing the various gods and subgods of the religion. Their three main gods are Brahma, the creator; Vishnu, the preserver; and Shiva, the destroyer.

Many gods and sub-god masks are sold on the streets to decorate homes. These are the same masks that are part of beautiful buildings in major towns and the dolls in this book. The mask figures shown in this book are made of papier-mâché or molded tin.

Inhabitants clothes are similar to Hindu attire in other countries, but each tribe has a slightly different style. The more money a woman has, the more jewelry she wears. The Tamang women wear nose rings.

215

#215. Three Spirit Dancer Marionettes: 12in (31cm); molded papier mâché masks; cloth bodies; molded clay hands and feet; (left to right) dressed in yellow, blue, green robes, with white, blue, red trim; all three have red highly decorated headdress; carefully molded faces with large bulging eyes; black thread hair behind the masks; 1992. These marionettes are the spirits of the many gods and subgods of the Hindu religion. **MARKS:** "Nepal" on seal in the middle of their white belt in front.

216

#216. ***LEFT to RIGHT:*** **Spirit Dancer (Possibly a Devil Dancer to Drive Out the Bad Things of the Year):** 8.5in (22cm); papier mâché face mask over cloth body; carved wood arms and hands; unusual dancer with gold mask face; yellow dress trimmed with sequins, bells, gold; blue apron; gray paper with mica scattered at neckline and on skirt; wooden base; holds a metal knife; very detailed costuming and painting; 1973. **MARKS:** "Nepal" written on base. **Nepal Farm Man:** 8in (20cm); all carved wood on base; beautifully sanded and finished; topi-type hat worn by the men of Tansan tribe; blue and white checked tunic and slim pants; carries a basket on his back with white straps over his shoulders; 1960s. **MARKS:** "Nepal" on bottom of base. **Nepal Farm Woman:** 7.5in (19cm); carved wood beautifully sanded and finished; black print flowered blouse; white belt; red polka dot pleated long skirt; carries basket on her back with red straps over her shoulder; 1960s. **MARKS:** "Nepal" on base. **Hindu Spirit Dancer:** 8in (20cm); body cut from flat piece of wood; pink and green costume with silver thread trim around the bottom; bodice ornamented with many gold balls on gold chains; bracelets on arms; gold trim around skirt; green metal face with pink crown glued on to wood; green cotton scarf attached to crown; the masked ornaments "tinkle" when the doll dances; 1973. **MARKS:** "Made in Nepal" on sticker on pink base bottom.

PAKISTAN

Pakistan separated from India and became a nation because of religious differences. This is a Muslim Koran following nation although people of other religions continue to live there. "Ursu" is the national language and is used in the schools, but many other languages are spoken.

Purdah for women is strict in the country, but in the city it is not followed as rigidly. Purdah means that women wear a long, usually black gown, called a "burqa" and a veil. Under the outer garment, the Pakistani women wear a tunic-like top with long pants.

Pakistan is northwest of India. It borders Iran, Afghanistan, and Myanmar (formerly Kashmir).

217

#217. ***LEFT to RIGHT:*** **Pakistani Hindu Woman:** 12in (31cm); papier-mâché head; body is straw stuffed burlap over armature; flannel hands with seams indicating finger; painted fingernails; Hindu red spot on forehead is red sequin; heavy black eyebrows and eyelashes; gold nose ornament; pink net veil trimmed with silver tinsel trim; purple rayon blouse with silver trim; dark purple print skirt with green and white print; heavy silver trim around bottom of skirt; 1994. **Pakistani Hindu Woman:** Same body and face as first doll; red tunic with green and gold trim; traditional Hindu pants; long red veil with gold trim. Crescent necklace on each doll. *Tanya Secrest Collection.* **MARKS:** Mohsin Factory, Ltd.

#218. Pakistan Muslim Girl: 16in (41cm); all cloth; painted face; deep blue tunic top and matching pants trimmed with blue; sheer veil over head and shoulders made of fine silk gold thread; leather boots; 1930s. *Tanya Secrest Collection.* **MARKS:** None.

218

219

#219. ***LEFT to RIGHT:*** **Lady with Sitar:** 7in (18cm); silk over cloth face and body; well sculptured and painted face; thread wig; star ornament in center of forehead; cotton shirt with gold trim; gauze-like blouse with gold stripes; silk veil with gold trim; green and gold bracelets on each arm; red painted fingernails; five-pointed star as a stand at bottom of sitar; 1960s. **MARKS:** "Pakistan Musician//Plays Sitar" tag underneath clothing. **Sikh Man:** 7in (18cm); cloth doll; painted face; outer wrap is dark cotton print with stars and geometric designs; black pants with the material pulled up through the crotch area; dark red turban wound high around the head; blue cotton shirt; 1960s. *Sandy Strater Collection.* **MARKS:** "Pakistan" printed on tag.

SAUDI ARABIA

The largest country in the Arabian peninsula is Saudi Arabia. It is almost entirely desert area. Both Kuwait and Saudi Arabia must depend on desalted water to obtain all their fresh water. Luckily they have extensive oil fields which allow them to live a normal, and even rich, life.

Saudi Arabia, for the most part, is a Muslim nation, and both Mecca and Medina, the Muslim holy cities, are in the kingdom. Men and women clothes are the same Muslim-type, desert clothes found in other Middle East countries. Since this is a very conservative country, women must wear black cloaks and veils in public at all times. Women cannot drive or travel alone.

The few dolls from Saudi Arabia are similar to other conservative Muslim dolls seen in other parts of this book.

Yemen is an independent country on the Arabian peninsula. *(See page 162 for a doll from that country.)*

Naomi, A World-Wide Doll Club Doll. See page 162 for further information.

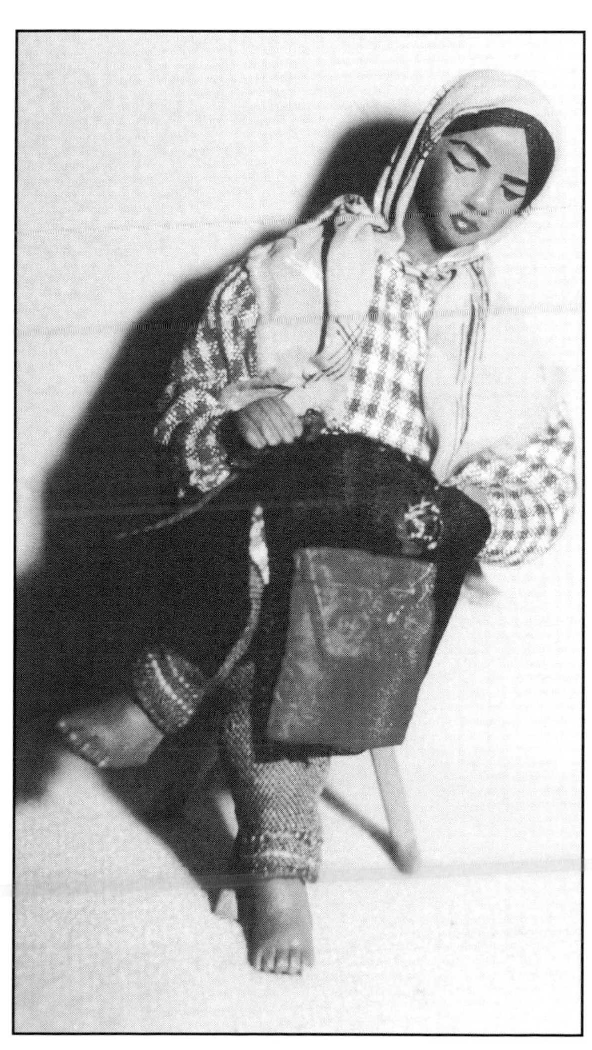

SINGAPORE

Singapore, a cosmopolitan city-state, consists of a main island and more than 50 outlying islands. Early in its history it was an inhospitable land with many mosquitoes and tropical sicknesses. However, because it was on a major trade route people came to live there. In the 14th century Java attacked the island, and most of the population was killed. However, by the 19th century people began to return to the island to seek trading location advantages. The British set up a post of their East India Company, and soon Singapore became a major port although living conditions were still crude. During World War II the Japanese conquered the city, and life was very hard. Eventually the war ended and the British returned.

The British finally gave them their independence in 1959. English is the business language, but some of the people of this "melting pot" island continue to speak their native language at home. They also use the Western-style dress for business, but they encourage their children to learn their own traditions and history, and some people still dress in their native costumes for special events and holidays.

Today Singapore is one of the cleanest and most crime-free countries in the world.

#220. Woman in Sari: 11in (28cm); papier mâché head; cloth body; green sari with much gold jewelry. There is really no Singapore national costume. Both of these dolls were purchased in Singapore. *Thelma Purvis Collection.*

220

221

#221. Singapore Girl: 7in (18cm); vinyl body; dressed in red headdress; blue blouse; black pants; lighter blue apron; carrying baskets on a pole over her shoulder; 1970s. *Carlton Brown Collection.* **MARKS:** "Singapore" seal on base.

SRI LANKA *(Formerly Ceylon)*

Sri Lanka is an island country formerly known as Ceylon. Situated off the south coast of India, it has a warm, tropical climate.

There are six main groups of people who live in Sri Lanka. About three-fourths of the people are Sinhalese Buddhists. About 20% are Tamil Hindus. Other people include the Moor Muslims, and Portuguese and Dutch Burghers. They dress according to the weather and to their religion. They like bright colors and many of them wear modern pants and shirts.

#222. ***LEFT to RIGHT:*** **Ceylon Devil Dancer:** 9in (23cm); all coffee wood; painted in bright red, yellow, blue, designs; painted open white shirt top and skirt; unusually large ears; open mouth with protruding teeth; bulging eyes; 1950s through the 1970s. These devil dancers were believed to chase away the evil spirits by dancing and making noise. Today they are used in shows for tourists. Different types of dolls have been made over the years.
MARKS: Made by//Arts and crafts//Ceylon.
Man in Sarong: 8in (20cm); molded hard plaster-type composition; dark-skinned man with gray shirt; white and beige striped sarong. 1960s. **MARKS:** "Ceylon" on shirt.

222

#223. ***LEFT to RIGHT:*** **Sri Lanka (Ceylon) Family:** all are carved wood and painted in various shades of black, gray, and beige. **Little Girl and Mother:** Girl 2.5in (6cm); Mother 4in (10cm); same gray dress with black trim and side panel; curls around forehead; black hat with gold trim. **Little Boy:** 3.5in (9cm); coat is painted with beige "u-shaped" dots; hat has slightly different decorations from his father. **Father:** 5in (13cm); coat has dotted "x's" for decoration. **MARKS:** "SERRV//SRI//LANKA" seal on mother.

223

SYRIA

Syria, a nation of the Middle East, is bordered by Turkey, Jordan, Lebanon, and the Mediterranean Sea. It has a wide range of landforms including the desert, mountains, and interior plateau.

The major language is Arabic. Kurds represent a 9% minority and maintain their own language. There are also Circassians, Turks, and others. Important religious differences with the Muslims divided the Sunnites, Shiites, and others. The major non-Muslim religion is Christianity, mostly Greek Orthodox. They also have a large Palestinian refugee group living in their country.

The population is well educated by Middle Eastern standards. There are many schools at all levels, but many rural people and women remain illiterate.

This country also has a petroleum-based economy.

#224. Syrian Breadmaker: 9in (23cm); papier mâché face; cloth body; blue print dress; holds loaf of bread; 1968. *Carlton Brown Collection*
MARKS: None.

224

#225. ***LEFT to RIGHT:*** **Lady:** 10in (25cm); cloth; tattoos on forehead, chin and bosom; blue brocade coat over white long dress; low neckline covered with netting only; black hat with white veil hanging from it with decorations near the bottom. **MARKS:** "Made in Syrie//Arouanie//Damascus".

Lady with Baby: 8in (20cm) lady; stockinette face that is needle sculpted and hand painted; nose decoration; cloth body; multi-colored dress made with scraps of material. 4in (10cm) baby; celluloid painted dark color; lady and baby are barefoot. **MARKS:** "Costume Syrian //sold by FR Saaden// Rest Haven Damascus"/. *Joe Golembieski Collection.*

225

226

#226. ***LEFT to RIGHT:*** **Syrian Man Playing Stringed Instrument:** 12.5in (32cm); cloth doll with soft sculptured face; real brown hair; dark green long baggy pants; beige and orange brocade shirt and jacket with long tail; long light green prayer shawl; green plaid Arab head covering; holding a string instrument; 1952. **MARKS:** "Made in Damascus, Syria" tag on tail of jacket.

Syrian Lady: 9.5in (24cm); composition face painted with kohl make-up; brown thread hair; wooden body; jointed arms; legs which can stand and walk; black Syrian-type dress with beautiful red hand embroidery; matching turban has with long gauze scarf. **MARKS:** "Syrian Lady" on tag. *Beverly Findlay Collection.* **MARKS:** None.

TAIWAN *(Republic of China)*

Taiwan, formerly Formosa, was a province of China. It is now an independent country with a Chinese culture. The religions, customs, art, and dolls are the same as mainland China.

#227. Fuji-Musume (Wisteria Maiden): 14in (36cm); painted silk mask face; vinyl body; black thread hair down to her waist in back; pleated pink skirt; rose brocade blouse; heavily embroidered panel with orange fringe around left side of waist; blue, yellow, red embroidered collar; black headdress with gold medallion in center; flowers on one side and gold ornament with red and green balls hanging from it; pink earrings; skirt has painted blue flowers around her feet; 1970s. The Wisteria Maiden is a Kabuki Dancer in a form of theatre that started over 250 years ago. Famous playwrights wrote stories of heroes and wars, of love and sorrow, of plain people and high-born, some bad people, and others who make one laugh. The stories are told through dancing, costumes, and special make-up. Every movement has meaning. The Wisteria Maiden and other Kabuki dance to the music of a three-string guitar-type instrument. **MARKS:** "Art Doll//Mandar in Brand//Made in Taiwan Republic of china.

227

228

#228. Old Man and Old Woman: 8.5in (22cm) each; papier mâché smiling molded heads with wrinkles in forehead; both have black hair with white streaks; man has streaked beard; woman wears black band on head; blue brocaded tunic; black silk skirt; carries red straw bag; man wears long dark blue Chinese skirt; black brocade jacket; carries a dark blue cane; 1982. All people of Chinese culture honor their elders, and people in Taiwan, Hong Kong, and China have dolls of old people. This couple happened to have been purchase in Taiwan. **MARKS:** "Chinese Doll" on box.

#229. ***LEFT to RIGHT:*** **Young Taiwan Farmer:** 13in (33cm); silk face; cloth body; rice cloth pant and cape; pink, red, white, and green cotton shirt and pants; holding a hoe; 1070s. A well-known award winning doll. *Sandra Strater Collection.* **MARKS:** "Made in Taiwan Free China//AWARD" sticker on base. **Old Taiwan Farmer:** 10in (25cm); painted clay face, hands, feet; stuffed papcr roll body; legs on wire; blue clay hat; dark blue smock; rice straw cape; white whiskers; carries two poles; 1950s. **MARKS:** None.

229

230

#230. ***LEFT to RIGHT:*** **Girl:** 12in (31cm); silk mask face; stuffed silk body; painted face; red cotton blouse and panel down front and back; dark blue skirt with yellow, green, and white tape decoration; dark blue pants with white tape decorations; silver sequins on front of dress; ornate red and green flower and feather headdress; multicolored large bead earrings and necklace; tiny blue bracelet with one sequin; doll is tall and slim; 1970s. **MARKS:** "Taiwan"//"Formosa" on base.
Girl: 7.5in (19cm); silk mask face; wood body; wire arms; dressed in the same outfit as the larger doll; holds a wooden implement for mashing something in the bowl on the base; 1970s. **MARKS:** "Huelien Ani Cultural Village//Huelien City Taiwan"

#231. Carved Wood Figure with Peach: 11in (28cm); camphor wood carved and painted boy; painted hair on top of head; large ears, wide nose; black painted eyebrows and eyes; dimples; open/closed mouth with carved teeth; all carved clothes; brown tunic; red carved sash; long green pants, tan shoes; hold a painted red, yellow, green peach; purchased August 1987, Chinese Handicraft Mart of Taiwan in Taipei. The peach is a Chinese symbol of long life. *Sherry Morgan Collection.*

231

232

#232. Taiwan Fisherman: 9.5in (24cm); composition head, feet, gauntlet arms; cloth body; excellent molded head with smiling face; wears straw hat and fiber jacket; blue suit; carries pottery jar; has wire line with two painted wooden fish; 1930s. **MARKS:** None.

THAILAND

Thailand is another Asiatic country which does not have any distinct cultures due to tribal migration and a varied terrain. While their costumes vary, they reflect the climate, religions, and arts which have developed during the centuries.

For many years both cotton and silk have been used for clothes. The work garments are cotton. Working women wear a *prasin*, a wrap-around sarong skirt, and a long-sleeved jacket. A sash may be worn over the left shoulder in the north. Special straw hats are worn for sun protection. The wealthy use silk for clothes which has been spun in Thailand for almost 2,000 years.

Folk art, especially doll art, has flourished in Thailand for many years. The costumes of the northern hill tribes have been part of doll collecting for a long time. However, now the people of these poor northern tribes are making their own beautiful dolls which are available through the U.S. Dollco Company and the Readshaw/MacMillan Trading, Ltd of Thailand. The sales help the hilltribe economy as they struggle to survive in a modern world. This is part of a world-wide effort to help indigenous poor people of many lands raise their standard of living, as well as show their beautiful art. Such examples of native workmanship can be seen throughout this trilogy of books on costumed dolls around the world.

Thailand is also known for the elaborate classical dance costumes which are sewn with heavy thread and decorated with jewels. Many have been made by the Chandavimol Company of Bangkok.

233

#233. ***LEFT to RIGHT:*** **Thai Classical Dance-Drama Dolls**. **Princess:** 6in (15cm); stiffened papier mâché mask face; cloth arms; wood legs; wood and cloth body; green dress made of metallic thread woven into cloth; trimmed with gold; gold papier mâché pointed crown. **Prince:** same construction and height as Princess; wears matching green costume with three orange panels trimmed with gold tape and sequins; 1970s. **MARKS:** None. **Thosaganth, The King of Longka:** 5.5in (14cm); molded, painted hard vinyl; blue and silver top and panels; pink pants; silver turned-up shoes; 1980s. **MARKS:** None.

234

#234. Lahu Standing: 12in (31cm); ornate headdress decorated with jewelry, beads, and tassels on the sides; black jacket; silver and bead jewelry around her neck; blue sash; multi-color striped skirt; carrying sleeping baby on her back; carrying bucket of fruit in one hand and a basket in another; 1993. *Harriet Beerfass Dollco. Boris Gelfandbeyn Photography.* **MARKS:** None on doll. A certificate of authenticity comes with doll.

235

#235. Akha Kneeling Doll: 8.75in (22cm); black jacket with multi-colored sleeves; short pleated dark blue skirt, metal beads; conical hat with yellow pom poms parted by metal and bead decorations; multicolored sash with silver disks and tassels; baby sleeping on her back has similar hat; carries basket of pomegranates on her right arm, and a quiver of arrows in her right hand; left hand holds a crossbow; 1993. *Harriet Beerfass Dollco. Boris Gelfandbeyn Photography.* **MARKS:** None on doll. A certificate of authenticity comes with doll.

236

#236. *LEFT to RIGHT:* Tai Classical Dance-Drama (Lakorn Ram) Part 1.
The Princess and the Prince: Most Thai classical dance-dramas have a prince as the hero and a beautiful princess as the heroine. There are exciting adventures, misfortunes, fights against demons and rogues, but eventually the prince emerges victorious and wins the love of the princess. **The Brahmin Dancer:** After the prince or princess has become a Brahmin in disguise, the usual practice is for him to perform a famous dance called "Shui Shai Brahm" displaying beautiful movements with appropriate music. **Thosaganth, the King of Longka (Ceylon):** The theme of this masked play is based on the classical Ramayana of Valmiki. The performers take the role of masked demons and monkeys. All the performers except the clowns do not utter any kind of sound, but conform their movements to the recitations and songs of the chorus. Thosaganth is a most interesting figure with many wives and 1,017 children, including two sons born of a female elephant and a daughter born of a fish. He usually has what looks like a "bow" in his hand. The costumes are very beautiful and glittery.

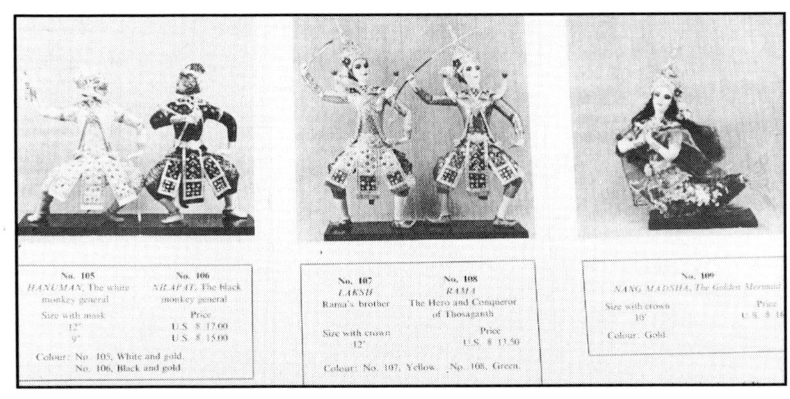

237

#237. *LEFT to RIGHT:* Tai Classical Dance Drama (Lakorn Ram) Part 2.
Hanuman the White Monkey General and Nilapat, the Black Monkey General: Hanuman is the son of Pra Pai, the Wind God, and Nilapat is the son of Pra Karn, the God of Death. They were reincarnated as monkeys to help Rama in his struggle against Thosaganth who abducts Sida, the wife of Rama. This abduction is the cause of a 14 year war between Rama and Thosaganth. **Laksh:** Tama and Rama's, Brother. Rama is the crown prince of Ayodhya in India. His stepmother uses his arm as an axle of the war chariot which enables the King of Ayodhya to continue his fight against the demon. He meets her demand that the throne be given to her son and that Rama, his wife Sida, and brother Laksh accompany him in his exile. The latter part of the story develops into their struggle against the demons. **Nang Madsha:** the daughter of Thosaganth and a fish. When Rama and his monkey army begin the construction of a stone bridge from the main land to the island of Longka, Nang Madsha is told by her father, Thosaganth, to command her army of fishes to remove the stones put into the sea by the monkeys. *Nang Madsha* is a unique doll – her upper body is dressed the same way as the Princess while her lower body is a fish.

#238. ***LEFT to RIGHT:*** **Thai Man:** 4.25in (11cm); stiffened jersey body; white and blue turban with printed Thai symbol. **Bangkok Lady:** 10in (25cm); papier mâché head; cloth body; black thread hair; black top with buttons down the front; black, yellow, pink, blue striped wrap around skirt; carrying a basket; wearing a straw hat; 1960s-70s. Tongkorn Chandavimol is founder and owner of Bangkok Dolls. Annually she produces about 5,000 dolls. **MARKS:** "Hand Made//Thailand//Bangkok Dolls" tag on large doll. "SEERV"seal on base of small doll.

#239. ***LEFT to RIGHT:*** **Princess:** 6.5in (17cm); cloth over armature body; high, pointed gold crown; gray and red dress with red robe; 1969. **Prince:** 7.5in (19cm) cloth over armature body; high, pointed gold crown; matching gray and red costume; panels of red and gold below the waist. The Princess and Prince are the heroine and hero of the classical dance-dramas of Thailand. *For more information see photographs on page 150.* **MARKS:** "Purchased in the shop of Madame Chandevimol (Bankok Dolls)."
Louise Schnell Collection.

238

239

#240. Karen PLO Standing Doll: 12in (31cm); white and red long dress embroidered in various colors; green headdress with red band; costume decorated with metal and bead decorations; carries a winnowing basket in her left hand and a hanging storage basket in her right hand; the red fringe hanging from her yoke is worn for ceremonial occasion. The tribe is known for their intricate weaving techniques. A smaller size doll has recently become available with similar costumes. *Harriet Beerfass Dollco. Boris Gelfandbeyn Photography.* **MARKS:** None on doll. A certificate of authenticity comes with doll.

240

241

#241. ***LEFT to RIGHT:*** **Hilltribe Collector Dolls:** 7.5in (19cm) to 12in (31cm); cloth over armature; all handcrafted; made in limited quantities; each doll comes with a certificate of authenticity and is numbered; ownership of each doll is registered both in the U.S. and Thailand. The seven tribes making these dolls today are the Lahu, Akha, Blue Hmong, White Hmong, Lisu, Mien, and Karen. **Blue Hmong Standing Doll:** 12in (31cm); pleated multicolored bands of skirt; one has intricate cross-stitch, for which the tribe is noted; black jacket with red cuffs; silver chains, pendants, and bangles decorate costume, ear, neck, and round hat with red pom pom trim on top; holding a "hon," a mouth and hand operated musical instrument producing a pentatonic scale; carrying baby on back with same style headdress; 1993. *Harriet Beerfass Dollco. Boris Gelfandbeyn Photography.*
MARKS: None on doll. A certificate of authenticity comes with doll.

#242. Lady from White Hmong Tribe: 17in (43cm); ceramic head, hands, feet; 1995. This is another version of the dress of the White Hmong Tribe from the first issue of ceramic dolls. Others include dolls from all six tribes, some men. **MARKS:** Each doll comes with a certificate of authenticity.

242

243

#243. ***LEFT to RIGHT:*** **Ongkot, the Green Monkey General:** 10in (25cm); all stiffened cloth; green removable mask over beautifully painted face; green silk arms; specially woven cloth with gold woven into fabric; red and gold trim with rhinestones decorating the collar, waist, and hanging panels. **Princess in Traditional Posture of Dance:** 10in (25cm); high gold crown with red flower; red bodice and train with beautiful gold trim; pants made with cloth woven with gold thread; 1960s-1970s. **MARKS:** "L SIAM ARTS//Made in Thailand" sticker on base. *Gigi Williams Collection.*

TIBET

Tibet is divided into three regions, Kham in the east, Amdo in the north-east and Utsand in the center. The costumes are basically the same, but they differ in detail. For both men and women the main garment is a *chubba* or *chupa*, worn folded across the body and held together by a belt.

The women wear the *chupa* longer than the men and have two blouses underneath. The drape and the hem have a contrasting color at the edge of the sleeve and the hem. Sometimes the women wear it to their ankles, and sometimes they wear it shorter with ankle-length pants.

The men wear their *chupa* ankle-length and sometimes wear a jacket over the basic garment. Both men and women have a high collar on the *chupa*. It is interesting that the young men tend to wear their *chupas* shorter. The men from Kham wear them knee-length, and those from Amdo wear them just below the knee. Large sheepskin and other fur hats are popular in this northern country. The costumes are similar to the Mongolian ones in design.

244

#244. ***LEFT to RIGHT:*** **Tibetan Lady:** 15.5in (39cm); all cloth; head has a molded oilcloth-type Oriental mask face which is heavily painted; sewn on ears; black wool hair drawn into bun in back; red hat that hangs down back like a scarf to ward off the wind; hat is lined with purple rayon; fur ear-pieces at each side; purple overdress split into four panels lined with gold trim; matching long green pants; leather boots on legs; yellow scarf around neck with red, white, black, and red print; triangular patch in middle. **MARKS:** "Dynasty Product (over a red crown);//Tibetan//I am a Tibetan." **Tibetan Man:** 15in (38cm); all cloth head has a molded oilcloth-type heavily painted Oriental mask face; sewn on ears; black wool hair; beige brocade hat with fur flaps; maroon side-fastening shirt with wide gold panel down front; leather boots attached to legs. **MARKS:** Tag is the same as the lady doll.

TURKEY

Turkey spans two continents, Asia and Europe. Even Istanbul, its largest city, is in Europe. However, most of the nation and the capital Ankara are in Asia.

Although Turkey has much in common with other Mediterranean countries, a leader named Kemal Ataturk brought it into the modern, moderate state of today. There are still areas where citizens keep the old ways, but they are changing rapidly.

While Turkey has other religions, Islamic ideas are still very powerful. Women continue to be viewed as inferior to the men. But since Ataturk forbid the veil for women and the fez and turban for men, fewer and fewer of Turkish citizens wear the costume of other Islamic nations. In the country areas many women still wear a scarf over their head and harem style pants.

Some festivals require special dancing costumes. In the spoon dance the male and female dancers are dressed in the colors of the rainbow, and the dance rhythm is clicked out with a pair of wooden spoons in each hand.

Men only dance the Sword and Shield Dance and wear battle gear of the early Ottoman warriors. The rhythm is produced by the clashing of swords and shields.

In the Black Sea area, they have the Horon Dance. The dancers are all male and dressed in black with trimmings of silver.

#245. Beggar Woman: 10in (25cm) seated; black hair; yellow scarf with red band around it; green and white shirt undergarment; red satin overblouse; blue coat; holding a stick; purchased in Kusadasi, Turkey; 1985. *Thelma Purvis Collection.* **MARKS:** None.

245

246

#246. Lady in Black Purdah: 10.5in (27cm); excellent wood painted head; cloth body; full cotton robe; net veil (shown "up" in picture) is pulled down when she goes outside her house; pink and white print dress with a fold on back for carrying a baby around the house; 1930s. *Sandy Strater Collection.* **MARKS:** "Turkey Woman" tag on dress.

247

#247. Hursi of Turkey: 11in (28cm); all cloth except for papier mâché mask face sewn over cloth; blue vest with painted design; blue pants with same design on side; red tasseled fez with white, yellow and brown band; holding a leather handled sword; black wool shoes; 1963-1964. One of Kimport's larger dolls advertised in the Kimport *Doll News* in the September-October 1963 issue. **MARKS:** "Turkey//5-29-A" tag attached to leather belt. **Woman from Turkey:** 10in (25cm); papier mâché head, hands, feet; cloth over armature body; orange, red, green, gold fez-type headdress decorated with sequins; lavender harem pants and matching sleeves; three-quarter length jacket of orange, green, white, purple, green colors with patterns in each stripe; red shoes; white net veil over headdress; a single wire protrudes from each shoe, and she stands nicely; 1965-1970. This was an inexpensive well made doll. **MARKS:** None.

248

#248. Turkish Pasha: 9.5in (24cm); clay head and hands; wood and wire armature; white headpiece decorated with small, turquoise sequins; red, white, green checked shirt; wide green satin Turkish pants; red felt coat trimmed with gold braid; wide orange, green, black, white belt with gold sword tucked in belt; holds dagger in right hand; 1966-1967. *Gigi Williams Collection.* **MARKS:** None on Doll; from the catalog of International Dolls.

249

#249. Turkish Traveling Man: 11in (28cm); papier mâché face; painted features with brown wool mustache; bald head; padded wire armature body; baggy blue pants; vest with long arm gold trim overlays; red, white, blue striped shirt; red paisley waist band; red and white "fez-type" hat; red pointed shoes on papier mâché feet; 1930s. *Beverly Findlay Collection.* **MARKS:** ERTUGRUL O ZSOY TURK EL ISLERI ATATURK BULWARI NO 144; ANKARA.

YEMEN

Yemen is a Republic in the southwestern part of the Arabian peninsula. It has been hard to find information about Yemen's history because until recently, outsiders have only been allowed in the capital city.

The climate is difficult because the coastal plain is a dry, sandy area with high humidity and temperature. The mountains are drenched with rain. The people, in many cases, were still living the life of the 12th century. Many have moved to Israel and suddenly found themselves in a different world.

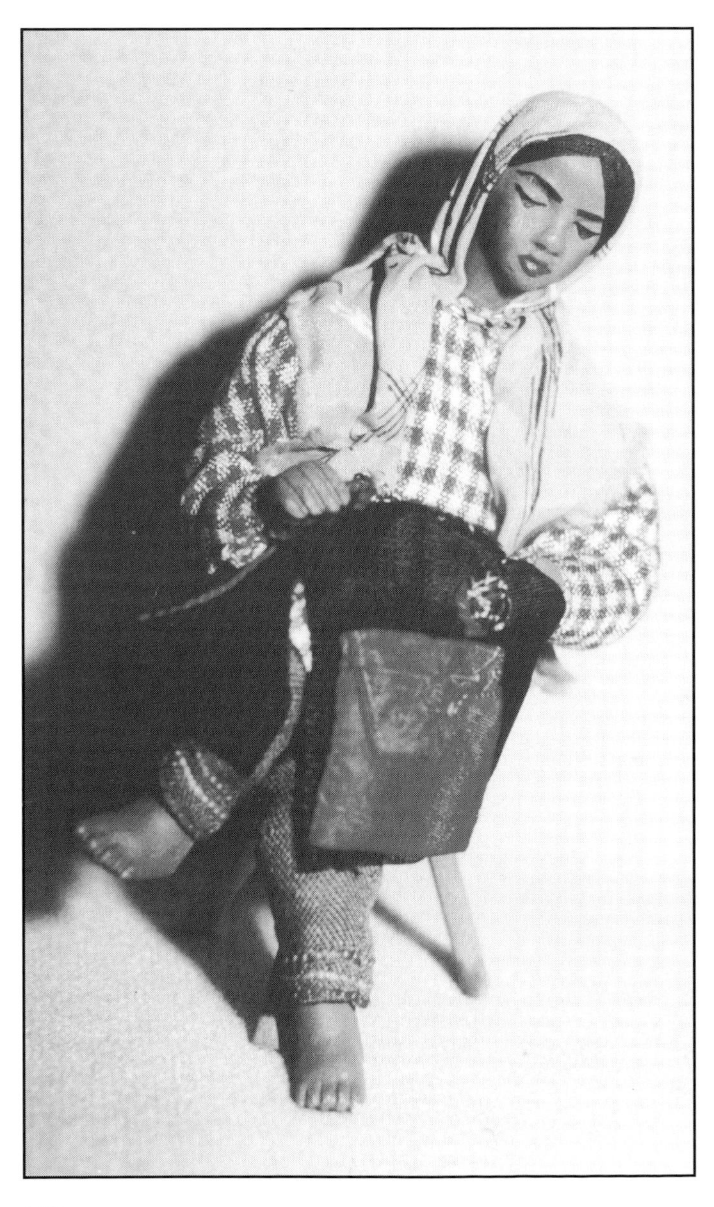

#250. Naomi: a World-Wide Doll Club doll; sitting on stool sewing; wearing the typical women's clothing which includes leggings under her dress. These dolls usually had a secret in its pocket, her's is an Israeli coin. Letter included explains the character's history. *Pat Moisuk Collection.* **MARKS:** None on the doll.

250

Mythological Symbols

Used on Chinese Antiques and Fabrics

Bats: Happiness.

Birds: The parrot warns women to be faithful to their husbands. The stork and crane are symbols of a long life. The magpie is a bird of good augury. The crow foretells evil.

Cornean Lion: He is the usual defender of Buddhist altars and temples. He is called the Dog of Foo or Dog of Buddha. He looks menacing with powerful teeth and claws. Actually he is a type of transformed lion. *(See page 62, bottom.)*
Dragons: This is one of the most familiar Chinese symbols. He is brought out at New Years and paraded through the streets. There are several types of dragons including winged, scaly, horned, hornless, or rolled up before rising to the sky in spring or diving into the water in autumn. *(See page 62, bottom.)*

Fish: A pair is a symbol of domestic happiness.

Flowers: Chrysanthemums are a very common decoration and the emblem of autumn. The peony represents love, affection, and good fortune.

Ho-Ho Birds: This is a symbol of elegance. It is a type of pheasant or birds of paradise. It would not hurt growing plants or living creatures. Although it lives in the high heavens, it comes to earth as a predictor of happy events.
Kylin: This animal looks like a type of deer. It has the tail of an ox, Hoofs of a horse, head like a dragon. It often carried in its mouth a scroll or other symbol. It looks terrifying, but is so gentle it would not step on any living thing.

Knots: Longevity.

Peacock: It is valued for his long feathers which designates official rank.

Peach: A symbol of marriage or longevity.

Pearls: Represents luck.

Shell: Prosperous journey.
All of these symbols may be embroidered or painted on the clothing of dolls as well as painted on porcelain, or other art objects. Watching for these symbols is another way of enjoying your Chinese dolls.

Price Guide

Illustration #	Description	Price
Afghanistan		
70	Afghanistan Couple	$20-25
71	Junubiwal, Pushtana ....Rare doll	40-60 each
71	Pushtana, Mullah ....Rare doll	40-60 each
Algeria		
1	Woman with Round Boxes on Head	$40-50
Bangladesh		
72	Women Snake Charmers	$15-25
Benin		
2	Benin Bronze Statue	$250-350
Botswana		
3	Herero Doll	$55-60
4	Botswana Lady	45-50
Burkina Faso *(formerly Upper Volta)*		
5	Upper Volta Mossi Doll .... Few samples available	$75-90+
Burma *(Mynamar)*		
73	Burma Lady	$10-15
People's Republic of China		
74	Chinese Boy	$65-95
75	Chinese Marionetes	20-30 each
76	Chinese Family	Few samples available for entire family
77	Hand Carved Chinese Ricksha	400-700+
78	Kneeling Warrior Tomb Figures	Not enough sample prices
79	Chinese Opera Dancer	125-150
79	Elderly Chinese Man	125-150
79	Horse and Rider	175-200
80	Chinese Nobleman	85-100
80	Madame Foo Wife of Merchant	125-150
80	Old Man	85-125
81	Flying Horse of Kansu	250-350
81	Opera Characters	100-125
82	Dragon	15-20
82	Monkey King Puppet	15-20
83	Six Chinese Character Dolls	600-700 all six
84	Chinese Ladies	100-125 each
85	China and Cloth Character Dolls	375-400 For all dolls
86	Noble Man	90-110
86	Noble Woman	100-150
86	Ricksha Pullers	50-75 each

86	Rickshas	$1,500-2,000 each
87	Antique Leading Character	2,000-3,000
87	Antique Servant	2,000-3,000
87	Nobleman	2,000-3,000
88	Chinese Bride	125-175
89	Monkey King	2,000-3,000
89	Young Man with Embroidered Coat	2,000-3,000
89	Young Woman with Embroidered Coat	2,000-3,000
90	Musical Girl	130-150
91	Monkey King	150-200
91	Old Woman	100-125
91	Younger Woman	100-125
91	Military Man	100-125
92	Cornean Lions	45-50 each
92	Monkey King and Emperor	200-300 each
93	Immortals	200-300 set
94	Mother and Child Pebbles Dolls	10-15
95	Door of Hope Amah and Baby	550-650 both dolls
95	Door of Hope Boy in Silk	600-700
95	Door of Hope Widow	550-650
95	Door of Hope Young Gentleman	550-650
95	Door of Hope Young Lady	550-650
96	Door of Hope Nobleman Groom	600-700
97	Mongolian Doll in Red	30-50 in box
98	Lao-tze	20-30
99	Young Traveler	30-35
100	Modern Boy and Girl	20-25 each
101	Doll from Xian	30-35
102	Modern Bride and Groom	30-35
103	Six Provincial Chinese Heads	25-30 set
104	Three Chinese Opera Masks	25-35
105	Panda	Not enough sample prices
106	Chinese Boy with Cymbals	50-75
106	Chinese Walking Boy	60-80
107	Mechanical Gymnast	15-20
108	Chinese Mechanical Baby	Not enough sample prices
109	Girl in Chinese Provincial Costume	35-45
109	Chinese Boy in Traditional Costume	35-45

Egypt

6	Egyptain Couple	$25-30 each
7	Mother and Two Sisters (set)	Not enough sample prices
8	Lady Water Carrier	25-30
9	Carved Stone Statue	35-50
9	Cotton Picker	25-30
10	Double-faced Egyptian	50-60
11	Mummy (Left)	Not enough sample prices
11	Mummy (Right)	Not enough sample prices
12	Nesting Mummies	45-55
12	Nesting Mummy of Nest-Nut-Neru	75-100

13	Shawabiti $30-50
14	Egyptian Couple and Woman....... 50-60 for all three

EITHIOPIA

15	Man and Woman .... $60-75 each

GHANA

16	Ashanti Fertility Doll $50-60
17	Male and Female Ashanti Fertility Dolls 20-30
18	Ashanti Fertility Doll 20-30
19	Lady Carrying Baby 30-35

HONG KONG

110	Beijing Opera Dolls.......... $25-75 each depending on country purchased
111	Chinese Family Dolls 125-150
112	Mao-type China Woman and Man .... 50-75 pair
113	Chieh-Chieh 150-200
114	Country Man 70-90
114	Country Woman 70-90
114	Woman Carrying Boy .... 60-80 each
115	Bow Bow 65-85
115	Chinese Girl 25-30
115	Chinese Woman 30-40

INDIA

116	Parci $35-45
116	Doll in Full Purdah 35-45
117	Christa Mandir Doll (Left) 50-60
117	Christa Mandir Doll (Right) 40-50
118	India Fish Lady 30-40
118	Hindu Woman 35-40
118	Punjabi North Indian Bride 50-75
119	Indian Rajah Boy 135-175
120	Bihari Village Woman 25-30
120	Bride from Marwar 25-30
120	Punjabi Bride 25-30
120	Rahasthani Farmer 25-40
121	Kerala Dancer 65-75
122	Brahan Lady from Madras 25-30
122	Hindu Woman Carrying Wood 25-30
122	Kashmir Muslim Lady 25-30
122	Rajasthan Lady 25-30
123	Hindu Lady with Red Dot on Forehead 25-30
123	Man from North India 25-30
124	Indian Military Band .... 55-75 for 8 dolls
125	Buddhist Sadhu (Holy Man) .... 70-100 few prices available
126	School Girl 25-30
127	Indian Horse and Rider .... 100-120+
127	Villager 35-40
128	Puppet (Left) 75-95
128	Puppet (Right) .... 100-125+
129	Ayah and Child 80-100

130	Indian Man and Woman Puppets	$18-25
131	Sikh Woman	30-60
132	Kashmir Doll	Not enough sample prices
133	Hindu Saraswati Goddess	50-75
133	Indian Man	50-60
134	Malan Woman	15-20
134	Man Snake Charmer	20-25
135	Kerala Dancer	30-40
136	Dhokra Lost Wax Brass Doll	35-40
136	Pathan Sikh from Northern Frontier	30-40
136	Sikh with Drum	30-40+

INDONESIA

137	Indonesian Goddess	$75-100

JAVA

138	Wajang Woman Puppet	$75-100
139	Wajang Shadow Puppets	75-100

BALI

140	Balinese Rod and Shadow Puppets	$30-35
141	Bali Bridal Couple	20-25
142	Witch Doctor	35-40
143	Balinese Votive Dolls	15-20

IRAN

144	Iranian Soldier	$50-80

IRAQ

145	Kurdish Man	$25-35
145	Kurdish Woman	25-35

ISRAEL

146	Lady Carrying a Large Jar	$20-25
146	Sabra Fiddler	15-20
147	Bride of Bethlehem (cloth)	40-55
147	Bride of Bethlehem (bisque)	235-265
148	Jacob from Jerusalem	25-30
149	Tzora	15-20
150	Hassidic Rabbi Carrying Torah	20-25
151	Man from Palestine	15-20
152	Hassidic Jew of Gur Community	20-25
152	Israeli Dancer	25-30
152	Member of Armed Forces	20-25
152	Orthodox Jewish Man	20-25
152	Sabra Settler	15-20

IVORY COAST

31	Colonial Doctor	$40-60
31	Yakuba Tribe	30-35

JAPAN

153	Girl's Day Festival (Yoshika Baker)	Not enough sample prices

154	Ichinatsu Ningyo	$150-200
154	Tiger	Not enough sample prices
155	Girl's Day Festival (Clay)	Very Old Not enough sample prices
156	Harukoma Doll with Horse	400-500
157	Boy's Day Doll	175-200
158	Boy's Day Samuri Warrior	200-250
158	Lady Musician	20-30
159	Boy's Day Emperor Jinmu	1,000+
160	General Riding White Horse	320-400+
161	Dance of the Seven Hats	12-25
161	Doll with Long Letter	12-15
161	Doll with Type of Spindle	30-40
162	Baby Boy Playing with Toys	50-60 Baby
162	Paperdoll Toy	7-10
163	Tenjjin	450-550
164	Japanese Baby with Extra Clothes	100-150
165	Meiji Bride	350-450
166	Ichinatsu Ningyo	700-1,000
167	Mayoke Doll	15-20
168	Dairi-Bini	125-150 pair
169	Crane and Tortoise (for both dolls)	250-300
170	Noh Play Figure	200-250
171	Hakata-Ningyo Representing a Noh Character	250-325
171	Ichimatsu Doll	40-50
172	Noh Actor with Puppet	50-75
172	Woman Serving Tea	200-250
173	Lion Dancers (set)	80-110
174	Gosho-Ningyo	200-800+ depending on condition
175	Takeda Doll	600-1,200 depending on condition
176	Hagoita (New Year's Doll)	35-45
177	Musical Sakura-Ningyo Cherry Doll	100-150
178	Kabuki Dancers	150-200 each doll
179	Japanese Squeaker Doll	30-50 depending on condition & size
180	JAL Stewardess	30-40
181	Ichinatsu Ningyo	150-200
182	Fukuruko	175-225
182	Japanese Nobleman	150-200
183	Wrestling Coach	150-200
184	Fisherman with Cormorant Bird	40-60
185	Musicians Playing a Koto	20-30
186	Tachi-Bini Dolls	Depends on size and quality
187	Daimyo Gyoretsu (including case)	400-500+
188	Mask – Dance Doll	50-80 depending on condition
189	Flashlight Kokeshi Dolls	35-40 each set
189	Kokeshi Nesting Doll	25-30
190	Kokeshi	25-30
191	Doll with 3 Wigs	50-80
191	Kokeshi Couple	25-30
192	Anesama-Ningyo	Usually a hobby; Dolls not sold
193	Mimikaki Doll	20-25
194	Izumeko Doll (Left)	5-8

194	Izumeko Doll (Middle)	$35-40
194	Izumeko Doll (Right)	20-25
195	Early Mitsuore	700-900

Jordan

196	Jordanian Man	$20-30
196	Jordanian Matching Woman	20-30
196	Jordanian Man	20-30
196	Jordanian Married Lady	25-35
197	Trans-Jordan Arab Couple	45-55
198	Jordan Aqaba Bazar Lady	15-20
199	Jordanian Musician	20-30
199	Jordanian Woman (Left to Right)	15-25

Kenya

20	Kenyan Doll	Not enough sample prices
21	Banana Leaf Doll	$12-15
22	Double Dolls of Samburu Tribe	20-30
23	Warrior From Kenya	25-35
24	Masai Female Doll	25-35
25	Kisii Mother and Child	20-30
26	Old Kenyan Man with Walking Stick	30-40
27	Young Girl	25-35
28	Kenyan Woman	75-125
29	Woman with Pot on Her Head	30-40

Korea

200	Korean Missionary Doll	$15-20
201	Two Korean Men Specially Dressed	25-30 each
202	Korean Woman	15-20
202	Korean Young Man	20-30
203	Korean Boy and Girl	30-32 each
203	Korean Lady	75-125
203	Old Korean Man	30-40
204	Lady Playing Stringed Instrument	25-35
205	Lady with Hand Drum	25-35
206	Korean Lady Dancer	15-20
207	Rice Straw Girl	15-20

Kuwait

208	Kuwaiti Couple	Very few sample prices

Laos

209	Kha Oma Doll	$40-50

Lebanon

210	Lebanese Man	$20-25
211	Lady	20-25
211	Man Beating Drum	20-25

Lesotho

30	Lesotho Doll	$15-20

Libya

32	Tripoli Dancing Couple	$20-30 each
32	Woman Carrying Water Jar on Shoulder	20-30

Madagascar

33	Elephant	Not enough sample prices
33	Lady with Baby	$40-50
33	Madagascar Man Going to Market	25-30

Malawi

34	Angini Warrior	$20-25

Malaysia

212	Bride and Groom	$30-35 each
213	Malay Lady	25-35

Mongolia

214	Mongolian Woman	$90-100+

Morocco

35	Moroccan Water Carrier	$35-45
36	Man	25-30
36	Woman	25-30
37	Moroccan Baby	300-375
38	Saudi Peddler from French Morocco	85-100
39	Business Man and Wife	25-30 each
40	Boy with Musical Instrument	5-7
40	Clothing Street Merchant	15-18
41	Woman from Rabat with Baby	60-80
42	Man on Camel	30-40
42	Water Seller Doll	30-40

Natal

43	Lady Stirring Food	$20-25

Namibia

44	Herero Lady	$30-40

Nepal

215	Three Spirit Dancer Marionettes (each)	$35-50
216	Hindu Spirit Dancer	35-50
216	Nepal Farm Man	25-30
216	Nepal Farm Woman	25-30
216	Spirit Dancer	35-50

Nigeria

45	Thornwood Basketball Players	$25-35
45	Thornwood Classroom	30-40
46	Thornwood Canoe with 3 Men	25-45
47	Ekpe Mask Doll	30-50

Pakistan

217	Pakistan Hindu Women (each)	Not enough sample prices
218	Pakistan Muslim Girl	$50-65
219	Lady with Sitar	40-50
219	Sikh Man	25-35

Saudi Arabia (*See Illustration 250.*)

Singapore

220	Woman in Sari	$30-35
221	Singapore Girl	15-20

South Africa

48	Ruella Artist Doll	$500-700+
49	Blanket Lady	150-200
49	Woman with Child	400-500
50	Ndebele Tribal Doll	150-250+
51	Xhosa Baby of Bantu Group	25-30
52	Ndebele Woman	Few sample prices 150-250
53	Bushman (San) Tribal Doll	Few sample prices 150+
54	Ndebele Tribal Woman	Few sample prices 150-250+
55	Cone Doll of Ndebele Tribe	40-55

Sri Lanka *(formerly Ceylon)*

222	Ceylon Devil Dancer	$20-25
222	Man in Sarong	20-35
223	Sri Lanka Family	35-45 all

Syria

224	Syrian Breadmaker	$25-40
225	Lady	25-40
225	Lady with a Baby	25-40
226	Syrian Lady	20-30
226	Syrian Man Playing Stringed Instrument	20-30

Taiwan *(Republic of China)*

227	Fuji-Musume (Wisteria Maiden)	$40-55
228	Old Man and Woman (both dolls)	30-35
229	Old Taiwan Farmer	25-35
229	Young Taiwan Farmer	25-35
230	Taiwan Girl (Left)	15-25
230	Taiwan Girl (Right)	20-30
231	Figure with Peach	100+
232	Taiwan Fisherman	75-100

Tanzania

Page	Item	Price
56	Tree of Life	$120-150
57	Skeleton Figure	220
57	Woman	45-50
57	Woman and Man Masai Heads	200 each

Thailand

Page	Item	Price
233	Prince	$20-35
233	Princess	20-35
233	Thosaganth	15-20
234	Lahu Standing	65-75+
235	Akha Kneeling Doll	65-75+
236	Tai Classical Dance-Drama, Part 1	No prices available
237	Tai Classical Dance-Drama, Part 2	No prices available
238	Bangkok Lady	25-35
238	Thai Man	8-12
239	Prince	15-20
239	Princess	15-20
240	Karen PLO Standing Doll	65-75
241	Blue Hmong Standing Dolls	65-75
242	Lady from White Hmong Tribe	75-100
243	Onkot, Green Monkey General	25-30
243	Princess in Traditional Dance	25-30

Tibet

Page	Item	Price
244	Tibetan Lady & Man	$250-300 pair

Tunisia

Page	Item	Price
58	Tunisian Holy Man	$40-75
59	Tunisian Girl	25-35
60	Arabic Girl	25-40

Turkey

Page	Item	Price
245	Beggar Woman	$50-60
246	Lady in Black Purdah	30-50
247	Hursi of Turkey	30-45
247	Woman from Turkey	20-25
248	Turkish Pasha	25-35
249	Turkish Traveling Man	45-50

Viet Nam

Page	Item	Price
202	Viet Nam Doll (1960s-1970s)	$45-75 depending on quality

West Africa

Page	Item	Price
61	Masked Figure	$100-125

Yemen

Page	Item	Price
250	Naomi	$25-40

Zaire

62	Boy with Bow and Arrows	$25-30
63	Old Zairean Figure	100-125
64	Primitive Doll	20-30

Zambia

65	Zambia Girl	$15-20

Zanzibar

66	Coffee Vendor	$40-50

Zimbabwe *(Old Rhodesia)*

67	Bahule (Guard)	$30-40
68	Father, Mother, Teach Son to Dance	150-200 all three
69	Garden Sculpture	Not for sale

INDEX

A

Addis Abba....................14
Afghanistan..............49-50
Afghanistan Couple......49
Akha Kneeling Doll ...149
Algeria.............................6
Algerian Woman Carrying Round Boxes 6
Amah.............................65
Anesama-Ningyo........119
Antique Chinese Opera Dolls 60, 61
Arabic Girl 40
Ashanti Fertility Doll......................15-16
Ayah..............................81

B

Baby 65
Baby Boy playing with Toys 103
Bahule...........................46
Balinese Rod 87
Balinese Votive Doll.....88
Banana Leaf Doll 17
Bangladesh 51
Bangkok Lady 151
Beggar Woman 157
Beijing Opera Dolls 71
Benin 7
Blanket Lady 34
Blue Hmong Standing Doll 153
Botswana 8
Botswana Lady 8
Bow Bow......................73
Boy 23
Boy with Bow and Arrows 42
Boy with Musical Instrument..................27
Boy's Day Doll...........100
Boy's Day Festival.....100
Bridal Couple 87
Bride..........60, 67, 76, 77, 87, 105, 131
Bride from Marwar 77
Bride of Bethlehem 92
Buddhist Sadhu 79
Burkina Faso 9
Burma 52
Burma Lady..................52
Bushman Tribal Doll....35
Business Man 27

C

Carved Wood Figure with Peach 145
Ceylon 140
Ceylon Devil Dancer..140
Cherry Doll.................113
Chieh-Chieh 72
China.......................53-73
Chinese Baby 69
Chinese Boy 53, 69
Chinese Bride...............60
Chinese Characters.......58
Chinese Family 54, 72
Chinese Girl 73
Chinese Lady................58
Chinese Marionettes.....54
Chinese Nobleman 56
Chinese Provincial Costume 70
Chinese Woman............73
Christa Mandir Doll 75
Church of the Holy Family.......................14
Cloth Character Dolls...59
Clothing Street Merchant...................27
Coffee Vendor...............45
Colonial Doctor............22
Cone Doll of Ndebele Tribe..........................36
Coptic Christian Man ...14
Coptic Christian Woman......................14
Cornean Lions 62
Cotton Picker................11
Country Woman 73
Crane 108

D

Daimyo Gyoretsu 117
Dance 37, 47, 56, 84, 92, 94, 99, 103, 109, 113, 117, 127, 134, 140, 147, 150, 155
Dancer from Traditional Chinese Opera 56
Dairi-Bini Couple.......107
Devil Dancer 134
Dignitary Holding Ceremonial Sword......7
Dhokra Lost Wax Brass Mother and Child......84
Doll Talk.................63, 92
Door of Hope Mission 64, 65
Double Dolls of Samburu Tribe 18
Double-Faced Egyptian Woman......................11

E

Egypt.......................10-13
Egyptian Couple.....10, 13
Eight Immortals............63
Ekpe Mask Doll 32
Elderly Chinese Man....56
Elephant.......................23
Emperor................62, 107
Emperor Jinmu 101
Empress 107
Ethiopia 14

F

Father.........................140
Father, Mother, Teach Son to Dance 47
Fisherman.....................58
Fisherman with Cormorant Bird.......116
Fish Lady......................76
Flashlight Kokeshi Doll 118
Fuji-Musume 143
Fukuruko 115

G

Garden of the National Gallery in Harare......47
General 102
Ghana 15-16
Girl 145
Girl's Day Doll............97
Girl's Day Doll Festival..........96, 97-99
Gofum..........................96
Gosho-Ningyo Doll 111
Groom.........................131

H

Hagoita Doll 112
Hakata-Ningyo 110
Hand Carved Chinese Ricksha 55
Harukoma Doll with Horse.........................99
Hassidic Jew of Gur Community 94
Hassidic Rabbi Carrying the Torah 93
Herero Doll.....................8
Herero Lady 30
Hilltribe Collector Dolls........................153
Hindu Goddess 83
Hindu Spirit Dancer ...134
Hindu Woman...............76
Holiday..........97, 98, 100, 101, 112
Hong Kong.............71-73
Hursi of Turkey 159

I

Ichimatsu 110
Ichimatsu Ningyo........97, 106, 114
India 74-84
India Educational School Kit................78
India Rajah Boy 76
Indian Man 82
Indian Military Band....79
Indonesia 85-88
Indonesia Goddess 85
Iran 89
Iranian Soldier.............89
Iraq 90
Israel.......................91-94
Israeli Dancer 94
Ivory Coast 22
Izumeko Doll.............120

J

Jacob from Jerusalem...92
JAL Stewardess 114
Japan 95-120
Japanese Baby 104
Japanese Doll Ceremony 98, 99
Japanese Doll with Three Wigs.............119
Jordan 121-123
Jordan Lady Purchased at Aqaba Bazar........122
Jordian Man................121
Jordian Married Lady.121
Jordian Musician 123
Jordian Woman...121, 123
Jubiwal 50

K

Kabuki Doll 103
Kabucki Dancers 113
Karen PLO Standing Doll 152
Kashmir Doll................82
Kenya 17-20
Kenyan Doll 17
Kenyan Woman 20
Kerala Dancer...............84
Kerala Man 77
Kha Oma Doll 129
Kimport 63, 92, 126, 131, 159
Kisii Stone Mother and Child 19
Kneeling Warrior..........55
Kokeshi.......................118
Kokeshi Boy Nesting Doll 118
Korea..................124-127
Korean Boy 126
Korean Girl.................126
Korean Lady 126
Korean Lady Dancer ..127
Korean Missionary Doll 124
Korean Woman...........125
Korean Young Man 125
Kuala 131
Kubucki Dancer 99
Kurdish Man 90
Kurdish Woman 90
Kuwait 128
Kuwaiti Couple 128

L

Lady 130, 142
Lady Carrying Baby on Her Back 16
Lady Carrying a Large Jar 91
Lady from White Hmong Tribe 154
Lady in Black Purdah ..158
Lady Musician 101
Lady Playing Stringed Korean Instrument ..126
Lady Stirring Food for a Meal 29
Lady Water Carrier 11

Lady with Baby 142
Lady with Baby Carried
on Her Back 23
Lady with Sitar 136
Lahu Standing 148
Laksh 150
Laos 129
Lao-Tze 66
Lebanese Man 130
Lebanon 130-131
Lesotho 21
Libya 23
Lion Dancers 111
Little Boy 140
Little Girl and Mother .140

M

Madagascar 23
Madagascar Man Carrying
Ducks to Market 23
Madame Foo Wife of
Merchant 56
Malan Woman 83
Malawi 24
Malay Lady 131
Malaysia 131
Man 122
Man Beating Drum ...130
Man from Palestine 93
Man on Camel 28
Manchu Nobleman-
Groom 65
Mao-type 72
Marionettes 133
Masai Female Doll 19
Masai Head 38
Mask-Dance Doll 117
Masked Figure 41
Mayoke Doll 106
Mechanical Gymnast ...69
Meiji Bride 105
Military 46, 55, 79, 89,
94, 102
Military Man 62
Mimikaki Doll 120
Mitsuore 120
Modern Boy 67
Modern Girl 67
Mongolia 132
Mongolian Doll in Red .66
Mongolian Woman 132
Monkey King 62
Monkey King Puppet ..57
Morocco 25-28
Moroccan Baby 26
Morroccan Water
Carrier 25
Mother and
Two Sisters 10
Mullah 50
Mummy 12
Music 27, 57, 68, 84,
113, 116, 123, 126, 142
Musical Girl 61
Musicians Playing a
Koto 116
Myanmar 52
Mythological
Symbols 163

N

Namibia 30
Nang Madsha 150
Naomi 162
Nara Dolls 108
Natal 29
Ndebele Tribal Doll 34
Ndebele Woman 35, 36
Nepal 133-134
Nepal Farm Man 134
Nepal Farm Woman ..134
New Year's Doll 112
Nigeria 31
Nigerian Classroom 31
Nobleman 115
Noble Man and Woman
Pulled in Ricksha 59
Noble Woman.............. 59
Noh Actors 108-110
Noh Plays 108-110
North Indian Antique
Style Horse and
Rider 80
North Indian Bride 76

O

Old Kenyan Man with
Walking Stick 19
Old Korean Man 126
Old Man 144
Old Woman 62, 144
Old Zairean Figure 43
Opera Characters 57
Opera Masks 68

P

Pakistan 135-136
Pakistan Muslim Girl 136
Pakistanti Hindu
Woman 135
Panda 68
Paperdoll Toy 103
Pathan Kikh 84
Parci 75
Pebbles Dolls 64
Primitive Doll 43
Prince 147, 151
Princess 151, 155
Punjabi 76, 77
Puppet 57, 81, 82,
86, 133
Purdah 75
Pushtana 50

R

Rajasthani Farmer 77
Religion 39, 79, 83, 85,
93, 94, 104, 135, 136
Rice Straw Girl 127
Ricksha 59
Ruella Artist Doll 33

S

Sabra Fiddler 91
Samuri Warrior 101
Saudie Peddler from
French Morocco 27
School Girl 80
Serry 21, 83
Shadow Puppet 86, 87
Shawabti 13
Sikh with Drum 84
Sikh Woman 82, 136
Singapore 138-139
Singapore Girl 139
Small Angoni Warrior of
the Bantu Race 24
Spirit Dancer 134
South Africa 33-36
Squeaker Doll 114
Squeeze Toy 66
Sri Lanka 140
Sri Lanka Family 140
Stewardess 114
Syria 141-142
Syrian Breadmaker 141
Syrian Lady 142
Syrian Man
Playing Stringed
Instrument 142

T

Tachi-Bini Doll 116
Tai Classical
Dance-Drama 150
Taiwan 143-146
Taiwan Farmer 144
Taiwan Fisherman 146
Takeda Doll 112
Tanzania 37-38
Tanzanian Carved
Ebony Figures 38
Tenjin 104
Tetami Dais 107
Thai Classical Dance-
Drama Doll 147
Thai Man 151
Thailand 147-155
Theater 109, 110
Thosaganth 147, 150
Three Spirit Dancer
Marionettes 133
Throne 107
Tibet 156
Tibetan Lady 156
Tibetan Man 156
Trans-Jordan
Arab Doll 122
Tree of Life 37
Thornwood Canoe with
Three Men 32
Tortoise 108
Tripoli Woman Carrying
Water Jug 23
Tunisia 39-40
Tunisian Girl 40
Tunisian Holy Man 39
Turkey 157-161
Turkish Pasha 160
Turkish Traveling
Man 161
Two Korean Men
Dressed for Special
Occasions 125
Two Women Snake
Charmers 51
Tzora 93

U

Upper Volta 9
Upper Volta Mossi Doll ..9

V

Viet Nam Doll 125
Village Woman 77

W

Wajan Figure 86
Wajang Woman
Puppet 86
Warrior 18
Water Seller 28
West Africa 41
Widow 65
Wife 27
Wisteria Maiden 143
Witch Doctor 88
Woman 26, 159
Woman Carrying
Boy 73
Woman from Rabat
with Baby 28
Woman in Sari 138
Woman Member of the
Armed Forces of
Israel 94
Woman Serving Tea ..110
Woman with Pot on
Her Head 20
World-Wide Doll
Club 92, 162
Wrestling Coach 115

X

Xhosa Baby of the
Bantu Group 34
Xian 67

Y

YaKuba Tribe 22
Yemen 162
Young Gentleman 65
Young Girl 20
Young Lady 65
Young Taiwan
Farmer 144
Young Traveler 66
Younger Woman 62

Z

Zaire 42-43
Zambia 44
Zambia Girl 44
Zanzibar 45
Zimbabwe 46-47

About The Authors

Both mother and daughter enjoy collecting dolls and learning more about dolls as a team. It was understandable that their research efforts and their love of sharing doll information would progress from writing articles for the leading doll collector's magazines to a book. Their first book, *Hard Plastic Dolls, Volume I,* and the hundreds of letters of encouragement that they received started them on a dozen year odyssey of writing a total of eight books. Both skilled researchers, Polly says "It just came 'naturally' that my daughter, Pam, and I write about the hobby we enjoy so much – doll collecting."

A retired junior high school teacher and Coordinator for Chapter I Reading Program for the Wickliffe City Schools, Polly devotes most of her time to writing. Pam currently teaches fifth graders and is a performing harpsichordist with a Masters in Musicology. Both women reside in Ohio.

OTHER IDENTIFICATION AND PRICE GUIDES BY THE JUDDS

HARD PLASTIC DOLLS, VOLUME I
An indispensible identification and price guide for every collector wanting to know more about hard plastic dolls of the 40s and 50s and their collectors' values. Over 600 photographs are combined with detailed descriptions to help the collector identify these dolls produced from 1946-1959. 312 pages. 5-1/2" x 8". PB. Item #H4638 $14.95

HARD PLASTIC DOLLS, VOLUME II
Learn about Alexander, American Character, Arranbee, Ideal, Nancy Ann, plus many more manufacturers! Discover how to identify hard plastic dolls by shoes and feet. 43 color plus 394 b/w photos. 256 pages. 5-1/2" x 8". PB. Item #H4703. $14.95

GLAMOUR DOLLS 1950S & 1960S
Featured are glamour dolls pictured in original costumes as well as many fabulous illustrations from vintage catalogs. Informs collectors of the characteristics of valuable glamour dolls. Over 400 photos. 256 pages. 5-1/2" x 8". PB. Item #H4639. $12.95

CLOTH DOLLS, 1920S & 1930S
Expansive photo guide to cloth dolls made by Lenci, Nora Welling, Chad Valley and many others. Lavishly illustrated with a bevy of beautiful photos plus packed with detailed descriptions to make identification simple. 47 color and 271 b/w photos. 256 pages. 5-1/2" x 8". PB. Item #H3979. $12.95

COMPOSITION DOLLS I, 1928-1955
A long-awaited, much needed guide to composition dolls aids collectors with those favorite postwar friends. 428 photographs display difficult-to-identify dolls augmented by a bevy of detailed text containing the most-up-to-date accurate values. An indispensable book for modern doll collectors. 130 color and 298 b/w photos. 8-1/2" x 11". HB. Item #H4389 $29.95

COMPOSITION DOLLS II, 1909-1928
Featuring the early prewar character dolls of 1909-1928, Volume II is the companion to Volume I. 302 photographs display difficult-to-identify dolls. Information is dedicated to the marks, characteristics and company stories of both the small and large manufacturers. Latest values. 135 color and 167 b/w photos. 176 pages. 8-1/2" x 11". HB. Item #H4691. $25.00

SANTA DOLLS & FIGURINES PRICE GUIDE: ANTIQUE TO CONTEMPORARY, REVISED EDITION
Discover valuable information about your favorite Santa collectibles from the information and price guide as well as the legends of Gift-Givers from other countries. Enjoy the different styles of Santa dolls, figurines, paper dolls and post cards and their costumes in 121 gorgeous color photographs and 146 b/w photographs. 160 pages. 5-1/2" x 8". PB. Item #H4702. (0-87588-420-2). $14.95

EUROPEAN COSTUMED DOLLS
The definitive price and identification guide for costume or travel dolls of Europe. The first book of a series. With 250 photos (over half in color) you will be able to identify costume styles and see the beauty of the unique European costume Dolls. These dolls are appreciating in value as people focus on their ancestry! Fascinating historical and cultural information. 160 pages. 6" x 9". PB. Item #H4741. $14.95